JUST
DON'T
BE AN
ASSHOLE

# JUST DON'T BE AN ASSH⊘LE

*A Surprisingly Necessary Guide to Being a Good Guy*

KARA KINNEY CARTWRIGHT

RODALE

NEW YORK

Published in the United States by Rodale Books, an imprint of Random House, a division of Penguin Random House LLC, New York.

rodalebooks.com

RODALE and the Plant colophon are registered trademarks of Penguin Random House LLC.

Library of Congress Cataloging-in-Publication Data is available upon request.

ISBN 978-0-593-13847-2

Ebook ISBN 978-0-593-13848-9

Printed in the United States of America

Book design by Jan Derevjanik

Cover design by Donna Cheng

10 9 8 7 6 5 4 3 2 1

First Edition

*Dedicated to my good guys.*

# CONTENTS

———

# INTRODUCTION

———

**G**OOD NEWS! IF SOMEONE GAVE YOU THIS BOOK, YOU'RE probably not a total asshole—yet. Some generous and very smart person thinks you have actual good-guy potential and wants to make sure you don't become an official full-fledged asshole.*

Maybe it was your parents, who want to see you get it together and live a productive life (i.e., get out of their house). Maybe it was a family friend or relative who fondly remembers how sweet you were before puberty turned you into a fiery ball of adolescent rage. Maybe it was "just a friend" who passed it off as a gag gift but secretly thinks you have boyfriend potential. Whoever it was, that person cares for you and wants to give you a little nudge in the non-asshole direction. Don't be an asshole about it.

———

\* We don't need any more of those, thank you very much.

If you bought this book for yourself, I am 100-percent certain you are not a complete douche canoe. You even get a few good-guy bonus points for self-awareness because you've realized that, way deep down, you may possibly have some asshole-ish tendencies.

For example, have you ever:

Ⓞ Gotten a technical foul in a rec basketball game?

Ⓞ Returned the family car with two drops of gas in the tank?[*]

Ⓞ Made out with someone, and then pretended you never met?

Ⓞ Dropped an F-bomb in casual conversation, only to realize that non-bro bystanders heard you loud and clear?[†]

Ⓞ Thought it would be hilarious to imitate someone of a different race or ethnicity from you?

Ⓞ Half-assed something important and disappointed yourself?

I'm not sure how to break it to you more gently than this: These are not things that good guys do. These are things that assholes do. Now, you may be surrounded by so many assholes that you're not sure what good-guy behavior looks like. And it's true that our society sends some pretty confusing messages about How to Be a Man. But I'm betting that someone in your life has been trying to warn you about your behavior and you've been, well, clueless. Fortunately, it's not too late to turn things around: Don't surround yourself with

---

[*] Some people around here have to get to work on time, you know.

[†] If people are gasping at your behavior, this is a clue that what you are doing is not a good thing.

jerkweasels. Make your own decisions. Learn how to read the signals people are giving you. In other words, just don't be an asshole.

Sure, asshole behavior can be appealing in the moment. It's funny (to you) and easy (for you) and requires no thought (on your part). But if you've had to stammer through an apology or come up with a pathetic excuse for yourself, or if you've ever been surprised by the unexpected (again, only to you) fallout after an asshole move, it may be starting to dawn on your still-developing frontal lobe that living the asshole life isn't all it's cracked up to be. You do not want to end up a permanent irredeemable asshole. Why not? Simply stated, the good guy generally comes out ahead and, in the long run, it's easier to be good.

How easy? Basically, there's one rule, and it isn't exactly rocket surgery:

### Rule 1. To Avoid Being an Asshole, You Need to Realize That There Are Other Human Beings in the World.

It's what everything in this short book comes back to: To avoid being an asshole, just remember that people who are *not* you are also humans. One more time: Other people are, in fact, *people*.*

Yep. That's the big secret to staying out of asshole territory, not ending up living in your parents' basement forever, and maybe even getting a date. You may *think* you already know how to do it, but for your own sake—for all our sakes—please read this book. Then read it a couple more times. It's short. Plus, there are handy charts.

---

* I didn't make this up, in case you were wondering. Old people—let's call them the Olds—refer to this as The Golden Rule: Do unto others blah blah . . . (You stopped reading this footnote at "unto," didn't you?)

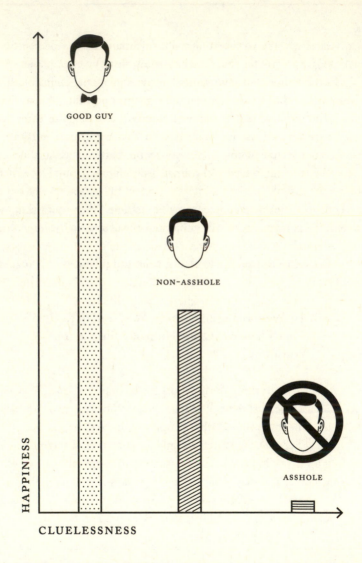

FIGURE 1: *Why You Should Get a Clue*

Why should you listen to me? See Rule 1: I am a person. I'm also a mom of two just-barely-adult young men. We've had our moments, but ultimately my family survived my sons' teenage years without burning down the whole neighborhood.* So I know that acting like an asshole doesn't mean you're a bad person. It doesn't even necessarily mean you're an asshole. What it means is that you don't understand how your man-sized presence is affecting other people in the moment and how *that* is going to affect *you* in the long run.

The goal of this book is not only to help you avoid being an asshole. It's also to show you how close you are to stepping it up and becoming an all-around good guy. I'm going to tell you everything I want my own sons to know as they go out into the world. Important things that will change your life, like don't give cheap chocolate and how to apologize without sounding like a politician.

Let's get started now, shall we?

---

* Hi, neighborhood. Sorry about all that yelling and door slamming. We're done now. Pretty much.

**1 /**

# DON'T
# BE AN
# ASSHOLE
# AT
# SCHOOL

SCHOOL IS WHERE YOU PROBABLY SPEND MOST OF YOUR TIME, so there's a good chance it's a prime contributor to your asshole behavior. I can understand why. Boring lectures. Useless tests. Arbitrary rules. Then there's the pressure to succeed, with your parents and your teachers constantly reminding you that YOUR FUTURE is at stake.

Factor in a bunch of hormonal teens trying to figure out who they are, and you've got something like a social experiment taking place inside something like a prison. At any particular moment, the whole operation is basically one social media post away from turning into a mob.*

But here's the thing: There's no way around it. You have to do school. You have to show up and do school every day until they hand you a cap and gown. Why? Because every employer is looking for doers, not quitters. If you have any ambition to make any sort of adult life for yourself, you need to graduate. If you graduate, you can get a job. If you get a job, you will have money. If you have money, you can someday move out. Living at home and letting your mom wash your underwear might seem like a good deal now, but at some point you will be faced with the reality that it is *not* the easiest way to get a date.

---

* And I'm talking pitchforks and torches, not adorable group choreography.

## THINK FOR YOUR DANG SELF

———

SCHOOL IS BORING and bad things happen when young guys get bored. Somebody gets a terrible idea, a couple other guys think it's hilarious, and then, before you know it, the whole gang is off and running toward totally foreseeable trouble and its painfully obvious consequences, ranging from after-school detention to "This will remain on your permanent record."

These guys aren't necessarily assholes. A mob usually includes some combination of assholes and non-assholes, although your ratios may vary. What mobs always lack is a good guy—one single good guy with the superpower of foresight and the bravery to step forward and make an absolutely incredible inspirational speech that changes hearts and minds, turns the tide, and saves both the mob and its victims from doom.

---

THINGS TO SAY TO TURN THE TIDE OF ASSHOLERY

Not a good idea, guys.

Ehh, let's not.

Nah, I'm not into this.

I was thinking we'd [*do some other less assholey thing*].

---

Although right now it may feel lonely to be the only person around who can think for your dang self, rest assured that this is a temporary situation. Picture a grown-ass man at work. Let's say he's sitting at a desk in a cubicle and his job is to scroll through spreadsheets all day. I think we can agree this is boring. And yet, *very rarely* does a grown-ass man pop up over the cubicle wall and whisper to his nearby buddies, "Psst. Guys. I hate this place. Let's eff it up!" It's even more unusual for other grown-ass men to pop up over their own cubicle walls and reply, "Yes! Yes! Yes! Let's do it! Let's eff it up!" And never once has a bunch of grown-ass men in athletic-fit dress shirts hit up Michaels for a dozen cans of spray paint and then dress-shoe-tippy-toed back to work to spray-paint M*****F****Rs and 69s all over their office building.*

***Hold the line against assholery.***
***It does get easier.***

---

* To the best of my knowledge. Anything's possible in Florida.

## PEER PRESSURE:
## ASK WHY

———

IT'S NATURAL FOR you to want to feel appreciated by the people around you. That's not a teenager thing, that's a human thing. But considering the current state of your developing brain and the sheer number of hours you spend at school surrounded by your peers, peer approval may well be the most powerful force in your life right now. That can be great if your peers are a bunch of good guys, encouraging you to do better and be better. The problem is, you don't have any say over who your classmates and teammates are, which means there are most likely some assholes in the mix.

Do not underestimate the influence of assholes. They can be relentless when it comes to peer pressure. Some assholes are not only tenacious but also very persuasive: It'll be great. It'll be fun. Everyone's doing it. You haven't done it yet? You're kidding. You're gonna love it. This is your chance. What's the big deal anyway? No one will know. How would they even find out? Blah blah blah.

When somebody is giving you the business about vaping,* cheating, drinking, drugs, getting sexy, or whatever, ask yourself: *What does this person have to gain? What do I have to lose?*

As you work through this formula, consider whether there might be something more behind your peer pressurer's motivations. Something unspoken. Something tactical. Something as in: "If we have enough people, the police won't be able to catch all of us." Or: "If we take this good guy along with us, maybe we won't get in trouble." Neither of these is a good reason for you to go along with

---

* In case this isn't clear to you and your friends yet, vaping is for douches. Someday you'll realize it was an idiotic fad—but also addictive and kind of poisonous.

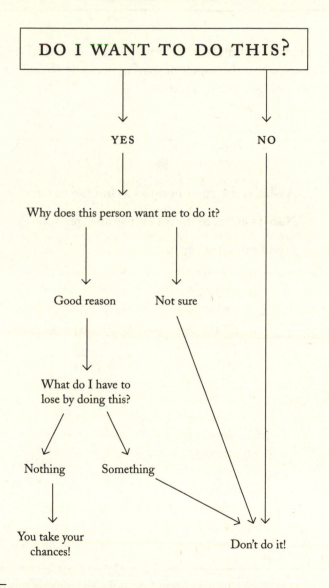

FIGURE 2: *How to Release Peer Pressure*

the plan. And neither of these things will turn out to be true. The bottom line is that the asshole pressuring you to do something stupid is not acting in *your* best interest.[*]

Assholes use their buddies as human cover.

Non-assholes make an excuse and get out.

Good guys just say no.

---

[*] Or his, but he doesn't know it yet. Maybe give him this book when you're done with it.

# HUMILIATION IS NOT ENTERTAINMENT

———

No matter how boring school is, no matter how tight your clique, how easy the mark, how big the pile-on—*no matter what*—humiliating another human being is an asshole move. Making someone feel worse is never the way to make yourself feel better. This is one of those asshole moves that will come back to haunt you later on when you develop a grown-ass conscience, which, assuming you're not a sociopath, is quite likely to happen.

In the olden days, the scale of humiliation that bored teenagers could inflict on one another was more limited because we would write our insults on paper* or pass them from person to person telephone-game style.† Aren't you so lucky to grow up in the digital age, when there are so many new and exciting ways to humiliate? Public posts intended to make sure someone knows he's left out. "Secret" polls and chats that *somehow* get screen-shotted and sent to the victim. (Oopsie!) Fake accounts that obscure the source of a rumor or confuse the target into sharing a confidence. So many new ways to bully someone! Plus, your language these days is so much more creative! Sure, we might have whispered that a boy was "scuzzy," but you kids have really upped the ante with "Go kill yourself." So clever! So advanced!

---

* For any history buffs out there, these elaborately folded affairs were called "notes."

† By telephone-game style, I mean on actual telephones, with only one line per household. It was bleak.

# ASSHOLE DEAD GIVEAWAY

### *"Go kill yourself."*

Stop that shit. Stop it. Some things are un-take-back-able. Some harm is undoable.

## THE NON-ASSHOLE PLAN

- When you see humiliation happening, don't join in.

- Unfollow accounts that are up to no good. And don't act like you don't know what they're up to.

- Unfriend—for real, in real life—people who prey on the weak. It's only a matter of time until they come for you. If you think staying on a bully's good side will protect you from becoming a target, you are mistaken.

- Don't be a bystander who laughs it off. Try saying something: "What's the point? Stop."

## NEXT-LEVEL GOOD GUY MOVES

- Lead by example. Interact with the targeted person as if that person is an actual human being, WHICH THEY ARE. "You OK?"

- Get help from a parent, teacher—any trusted adult—before it gets out of hand. Do *not* wait until it becomes "a matter for the authorities."

# TEACHERS ARE PEOPLE, TOO

——

**TALKING ONE WAY** with friends and another way at school doesn't make you a kiss-ass or two-faced. People with roots in two cultures do this all the time, and only assholes fault them for code switching to communicate effectively in different situations. If you're thinking, "I am who I am and if they don't like it, too bad," you're right. It's too bad. For you. Because your teachers are humans, grading is subjective, and if your teacher misinterprets your language as ignorance or disrespect, you're the one who's going to suffer, fairly or not. Plus, it's not that hard!

| BRO CODE | SCHOOL CODE |
|---|---|
| bruh | sir/ma'am/your teacher's actual name |
| Nah. | No, thank you. |
| Huh? | Could you please repeat that? |
| Grunt. | Yes, please. |

TABLE 1: *How to Impress Your Teachers Without Really Trying*

And watch your tone. What you're going for is respect, not disdain.* If you view your teacher or professor as someone who works

---

* It's a shame, really. As I've experienced firsthand, teenagers are incredibly gifted at withering disdain—yet so rarely rewarded for it.

for you, you are an asshole. A better to way to view your teacher is as the person who can fail you for being an asshole. The *best way* to look at your teacher is as your practice boss.

Unless you're cooking up some kind of entrepreneurial plan,[*] you are going to have a boss. Even someday when you get to be the boss, you'll have a bigger boss. Every boss has a boss. It's true! The CEO reports to the board. The board reports to the shareholders. There's no way around it.[†]

The good news: If you manage to survive high school, and then if you go on to college, you're going to end up having, let's say, one hundred different teachers. Some will be kind, some will challenge you, some will inspire you, some will be pointless, some will be assholes, and some will act like they want to be your best friend.[‡] It's good to learn how to work with and for all these kinds of people. Here's your job for now: Figure out your teacher's expectations. Meet the expectations.

Speaking of expectations, only assholes think the rules don't apply to them. A deadline is not a negotiation, no matter how charming you think you are. A deadline is the actual time that you need to *turn in* your assignment. Something that happens with strange frequency is that students do their work and just as they are about to turn it in on time, some freak-unexpected-completely-not-

---

[*] *Not meth. Not meth. Please don't be meth.*

[†] Attention, aspiring entrepreneurs, athletes, gamers, and artists: Are you under the impression that you don't need to finish school because you'll never work for the Man? Good luck with that. Because even with your talent, you are going to need a considerable amount of luck. Like, struck-by-lightning-multiple-times-and-lived levels of luck. So maybe don't give up on school just yet.

[‡] Watch out for those, please. No right-minded adult needs teenage peers. I promise you, this is not as cool as it seems.

the-student's-fault thing happens and prevents the assignment from reaching the teacher's in-box. What are the chances?

High school teachers and college professors have hundreds of students. As bad as they might feel about your Freak Thing (which totally really happened), they don't have time to deal with everybody's Freak Thing on every assignment. The department director or principal is breathing down your instructor's neck, hassling him or her to get the grades in on time.* That's why the classroom contract or syllabus you got on the first day says, basically, "Do your work on time. I don't care about your Freak Thing."

Something else you should know about human teachers: They generally like teaching. It may not seem like it, but that's usually because they're fed up with other non-teaching administrative bullshit. What gets them up in the morning is not the big bucks. It's educating young people—not just on the Pythagorean theorem but on critical life skills, like how to get out of quicksand. If you need help, or you're struggling, or if you waited so long that now you're totally screwed, let your teacher or professor know what's going on and ask for help—in complete sentences. Make it clear that you understand this is your problem, not theirs, but you are still hoping they will consider helping you. Send the email. (TIP: Start it with "Dear Ms. ____," not "Hey teach!") Show up at office hours. Maybe don't wait until after the deadline, but it's always better to communicate than not to. Remember, teachers are humans with a subjective slush fund of points they can't help but award more generously to students who at least appear to care. So, if you've been blowing off a class, the first line of your desperate email to the instructor had better include the words "I'm sorry."

---

* Everybody has a boss!

# DON'T BE YOUR OWN
# WORST ENEMY

———

To REVIEW:

1. The goal of school is to get the heck out of school,
   preferably by graduating, so you can get a job that pays
   money, move out, wash your own underwear, and get a
   sex life.[*]

2. The best way to graduate is to not fail.

3. The best way to not fail is to do the work.

Granted, there are more fun things to do than schoolwork. It's
easier to play video games than to write a paper. *Is it, though?*

If you choose gaming instead of writing a paper, or if you
choose mostly gaming but squeak out a shitty paper, you'll have to
deal with the consequences: anxiety about procrastinating and/or
doing poorly, dealing with your disappointed teacher and screaming
parents, working harder to bring up your grade, begging for extra
credit, etc. So maybe doing your schoolwork is easier than gaming?

Do you need a moment to recuperate from that mind-blowing
realization?

Now that you've decided to do the work, you're going to
need some discipline. Not the familiar screaming-parent "You're
grounded" kind of discipline. Self-discipline. You being the self in

———

[*] Or even just a second date.

question. The bad news on this one is that the cards are stacked against you in a way they weren't for your parents.

Social media, gaming, streaming video—all these things have been designed by evil geniuses to affect your brain in a way that makes them hard to turn off. It's not a coincidence that when you get a notification, you instantly tap it to take a quick peek and don't look up until an hour later. It's no accident that there's always another game level and that you just happen to know that the next level is where it really starts to get good. Being unable to turn off a screen doesn't make you weak. It makes you a human person with a human brain. But it also means that you are the only person who can discipline yourself not to turn on the screen when you have work to do. A few ideas:

* *Make sure you're the boss of your phone and your phone is not the boss of you.* Turn off the notifications. Beeps and buzzes don't decide when you look. *You* decide when you look. If you have to, put your phone in another room to get some work done.

* *If you need your phone or computer to do an assignment, get one of those apps that locks down your social and gaming sites while you're working.* If you find that idea scary, try it for fifteen minutes. You can do anything for fifteen minutes. Then try it for thirty. Then do it for the two hours you need to study to ace your test.

* *If you're in college, go to class.* Missing class is a worst-case scenario that will give you nightmares for the rest of your life. Ask any college graduate. We *all* have a recurring nightmare where we have to take a final exam for a course we never attended.

✳ *If you go to class, keep your phone in your pocket.* Otherwise, you're wasting your time. And somebody's money. Do you have any idea what college costs?!\* If you're in college, do some of that fancy math and figure it out:

_____ **Semester tuition**

÷

_____ **Number of courses you're taking**

÷

_____ **Weeks in a semester**

÷

_____ **Number of times the class meets per week**

=

_____ **How much it costs to sit in one class**

**(Please label your answer in dollars and,
for extra credit, specify who earned them.)**

Think about that number every time you're tempted to whip out your phone in class. If you can be the boss of your phone, maybe someday you'll be an actual boss capable of independent thought instead of some asshole in the back of the room snorting at texts about last night. (P.S. Your professor can tell the difference between you taking notes and you scrolling the internet.)

---

\* If you know dang well what college costs because you're paying your own way, you are a *truly* impressive individual. Keep going!

# DON'T CHEAT

——

ACADEMIC HONESTY IS a non-negotiable. It's the one violation that will instantly turn emailing-the-principal helicopter parents into nature-show parents of the eat-their-young variety. Trusted friends will crack under questioning and flip on you faster than your instructor can post a zero. Teachers, professors, principals, and deans do not play when it comes to cheating. Schools have expelled students for violations of the honor code at whiplash speed.

If you feel tempted to cheat because you're overwhelmed by the pressure to succeed, just imagine the faces of the very people you're trying *not* to disappoint when they find out you cheated: It will be like that painting *The Scream,* but in live-action 3-D with the sound turned all the way up forever. In other words, it's a nightmare scenario.

Instead, if you're in over your head, talk to your instructor. Talk to your advisor. Talk to your parents. If you have the kind of parents who make this kind of thing hard to talk about, text instead:

*Dad. I'm in trouble.* [Now, wait one whole minute]

*I've been too scared to tell you.* [Wait thirty seconds, the longest thirty seconds of your poor dad's life]

*I'm not getting pre-calc.*

He'll be so happy no one is pregnant, it'll seem like no big deal. There are always options (peer tutoring? faculty support? a different course?) and, I promise you, none of them means you're a worthless failure. You make an adjustment and you move forward.

Oh, and if you're perfectly capable of doing the work but you're considering cheating because you think the assignment is a useless waste of your time, you are grossly overestimating your importance, your abilities, or both. This delusion can lead to a series of unfortunate events (failure, tarnished reputation, missed opportunities) that can ultimately result in extended basement dwelling. Go back to the first page of this chapter and start over.

## YOU CAN DO IT

———

ONE BIG PROBLEM with school is that it isn't for everyone, but it's required for everyone. In other words, not everybody is cut out for school, but everybody needs school to (repeat after me) get a job and get money so he can move out and wash his own underwear.

Sometimes people act like assholes because they just can't do school. If this is you—if you hate school with the fiery passion of 10,000 suns and every day you make sure everybody knows it—the first step is to stop being an asshole. You're not the only one who feels this way. It may seem like it, but that's only because school is all about fitting in and that makes the picture deceiving.

I'm not saying everyone is taking Adderall or Prozac, but there are plenty of guys your age who look just like everybody else and are wired in a way that makes school harder. People you know may have anxiety, depression, or ADHD, or they may be on the autism spectrum. There's just no way to know what's going on inside other people's heads.

What is important for you to know is what's going on inside your own head. Rather than giving up on school or sabotaging yourself, a better plan would be to find out why your brain makes school terrible. You may just be having a tough moment or you may need some help. Ask your parent or school counselor for help finding a therapist or doctor you can talk to. It can be a scary thing to do, but if you do it, people a lot smarter than me can help you figure out what needs to happen to make school work for you. You might have to work harder and longer than other people—and that sucks—but you can do it. And when other people see you doing it, they'll know they can, too.

# DON'T
# BE AN
# ASSHOLE
# TO YOUR
# FRIENDS

**L**ET'S LEAVE THE MOB BEHIND AND MOVE ON TO SOMETHING easier to deal with: your close friends. Friends understand each other. They root for each other even when they're jealous. They tell the truth. They don't walk away when things get hard. They forgive, and they never forget.*

Is that only two or three people? That's fine. Twenty people? That's fine, too.

Here's the thing about friends: It's so easy to be with them that you may get the idea that you're in an anything-goes, no-obligation, no-consequences zone. If you're the type of "friend" that shits all over everyone and expects them to laugh it off time and time again, you are an asshole. And for a little while people may be fine with keeping an asshole around for entertainment, or because it makes them feel better about themselves. This is especially true in a long-term hostage situation like high school, a sports league, or the dorm. But when everyone starts moving up and out—and this day is coming sooner than it may seem to you right now—they'll get to choose their own friends, and (Spoiler Alert!) if you're an asshole, they're not going to choose you.

---

* A critical protection against recurring dumb behavior of the never-told-your-parents variety.

## BE LOYAL

———

I DON'T NEED to tell you that it's important to be loyal to your friends. Guys your age are so serious about keeping confidences that a mom can start to wonder if her sons' friends are in the witness protection program or possibly the Mafia.*

For good guys, loyalty means more than keeping secrets. It also means you have your friends' backs—that you're going to step up and stop your friends from making idiot moves that are clearly going to go badly. This can require a little bluntness.

> FRIEND: *Let's jump off the roof and dunk on the way down! Where's your GoPro?*
>
> GOOD GUY: *No.*

It also means that sometimes good guys have to look into the future and determine when an idiot move aimed at someone else is going to boomerang back and smack a friend right between the eyes. In these cases, you need to stop that boomerang launch while keeping it clear that you're always and truly on your friend's side.

> FRIEND: *She's sorry? I'll make her sorry she ever met me. I have nudes.*
>
> GOOD GUY: *Not a good look, dude. Delete and move on. Gimme your phone. I'll do it.†*

———

\* My own sons spent years furiously texting "No one!" about "Nothing!" Seriously, do you guys take an oath or something?

† It's also potentially criminal, depending on your friend's age and the girl's age, but it's probably not the ideal time to research this when your friend has his finger on SEND.

It gets tougher when a friend is in trouble in a way you're just not able to address on your own. In these (hopefully rare) situations, having your friend's back may mean sharing a confidence with someone in a position to provide real help. Whether to reach out will be a tough decision—you may even fear it will end your friendship—but loyalty means doing what's best for your friend, not what's most comfortable for you. If your friend needs ongoing help with health, safety, or permanent record–type business, you're going to have to talk with someone on Team Olds. It doesn't have to be a parent. You can touch base with a counselor or trusted teacher. You can call a doctor (even your pediatrician!) for confidential advice. You can Google "help for people with [*whatever the problem is*] in [*the place where you live*]" to get some options. Don't be an asshole who does nothing to save a friend who's drowning. He's counting on you to throw him a line, even if he doesn't know it.

**Don't just stand there.**
**Do something.**

## SHOW UP

—

HIGH SCHOOLERS ARE *constantly* changing plans. They'll deploy from various locations with only the sketchiest plan for where they're going or who will be there, yet still somehow manage to storm places like Chipotle with military precision and in numbers that can terrify toddler moms and burrito makers alike.

Warning: On-the-fly negotiation of each and every social gathering is a high school–specific activity. More mature individuals, such as college students, have less time to spend texting last-minute changes of plans due to life's more rigorous demands.* Once you get past high school, only assholes bail and flake. Non-assholes settle on a plan before everyone heads out. Good guys show up at the place on time.

Showing up for your friends amounts to more than making it to the party before everyone else is ready to leave. It's a subset of an absolutely critical good guy rule: **Do what you say you're going to do.** I'm sure you've heard the Olds saying things like "A man's word is his bond." What Pops is trying to tell you is that it matters whether you keep your word—every time, even to your friends, even if they say it doesn't, even if you have an excuse.

People need to be able to count on other people. That's how human societies work. At the same time, trust is very fragile. The Olds have a saying for this, too: "Fool me once, shame on you. Fool me twice, you're grounded indefinitely and don't even ask me about the car."† Before you ask someone "Why don't you trust me?" ask yourself why they should.

---

* And by "rigorous demands" I mean naps. College entails a surprising number of naps.

† Or is that one just me?

## R-E-S-P-E-C-T

———

**WHEN YOU'RE INVITED** into a friend's home, have some respect for your hosts, their belongings, and the other guests. It's going to be hard for you to maintain friendships if you get blacklisted from entering the residences of everyone you know, so look around for clues that might help you assess the realm of socially acceptable behavior. For example, if nobody else is crushing cans on their foreheads, this probably isn't the occasion when you should choose to demonstrate that particular talent. Take a moment to size up the food and beverage offerings and consider the number of people present before you eat *all* the food and drink *all* the drink. And be careful of the drywall, please.

## *ASSHOLE DEAD GIVEAWAY*

*Leaves a friend's home in need
of professional cleaning or a trip
to Home Depot.*

Don't overstay your welcome, either. You'd be surprised how easy it is to go from good guy to asshole just by hanging around a tad too long.

## HOW TO AVOID PAINFULLY AWKWARD EXITS

IF ANY OF the following things is happening, you need to get going:

* *food being cleared away*

* *a change in lighting*

* *stretching and yawning of any kind**

* *"Whose coats are these?"*

* *someone walking around with a trash bag*

TIP: If you've stayed long enough to see the trash bag, congratulations! You're on trash duty, too. Get up and get cleaning.

---

* If you are at someone's parents' house and the Olds traipse through in comfy sweats or pajamas, GET OUT.

## "JUST KIDDING" IS NO DEFENSE

———

THE JUST KIDDING Defense works pretty great in middle school, but it's time to knock it off. Nobody thinks your antics are innocent, clever, or cute. That's kid stuff. You and your friends may feel like kids when you're goofing around together, but you look and sound like men to everybody else. You're taller than the rest of us, and your voices are deeper and louder than you think. You doofuses are intimidating.

When you're in the guy-friend mind meld, riffing on comedy bits and cracking each other up, the people at the next table have no idea you're just kidding around. Your devastating impression of a racist sounds an awful lot like an actual racist. Nobody gives a crap whether you're "only" being inappropriate, insensitive, or stupid. It all looks like capital-*A*-Asshole, so don't be surprised if you're called on it.

*Gold standard for good guy behavior:*
*No explanation required.*

## ON THE MONEY

———

THE ONE THING you can be sure of when it comes to money is that every person you meet has a unique perspective on it. A close friend with the same upbringing and same economic status as you (as far as you know, and you never really know) may have completely different rules for saving, spending, lending, and even talking about money.

Still, when a friend doesn't have the cash to come along, it sucks for everybody. Sucks for him to say he can't afford it. Sucks for you to go on ahead without him. If you have the means, you can certainly offer to pay his way, but don't expect the money back. Make clear (to yourself, especially) that it's a gift, not a loan. If he's a good guy, he'll pay you back anyway, as soon as he can. If you're a good guy, you won't expect him to.

If you're the one short on funds, don't make it awkward. Just say you can't make it. Some people will always have more than you. Some people will always have less than you. It's OK, really. Don't let someone pay your way unless you're sure you can pay it back. Pay it back as soon as you have the money. Don't wait until you have cash. Money transfer apps exist for a reason.

*Important face-saving bonus tip:* If you do ask a friend for a loan, be prepared to take no for an answer the first time.

## *ASSHOLE DEAD GIVEAWAY*

*Asks again to borrow money after
a friend has said no.*

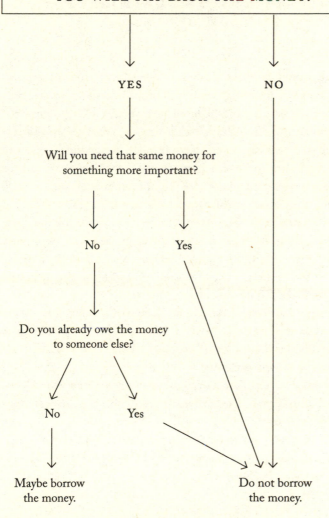

**DO YOU HAVE A PLAN FOR HOW AND WHEN YOU WILL PAY BACK THE MONEY?**

YES

NO

Will you need that same money for something more important?

No

Yes

Do you already owe the money to someone else?

No

Yes

Maybe borrow the money.

Do not borrow the money.

FIGURE 3: *How Not to Be a Deadbeat*

# MAINTAIN SITUATIONAL AWARENESS

——

THE MILITARY VERSION of Rule 1 is called "situational awareness." In that context, knowing where you are, understanding the situation's circumstances, and being able to predict what might happen next have life-and-death consequences. What this means for you and your friends as you move through the world is that you need to be aware that other humans exist, those humans can see you and hear you, and people often react in unpredictable ways. Do you think that family at the next table is just going to sit there and listen to you say the F-word twenty times? Do you think the manager has nothing better to do than clean up the thirty-two-ounce soda you spilled while you were horsing around? Oh, look, a couple of police officers just popped in to grab a bite. This deployment isn't going to end well, is it?

When you become aware that you and your friends are being perceived as assholes, you need to do something. You don't need to make a big deal out of it. If people start staring at you doofuses (or, better, *before* people start staring at you doofuses), say a quiet word or two: *"Dudes. People."* You can also try flashing your friends a Ninja Laser Stare of Instant Death.* If all else fails, relocate. Just keep calmly saying "Let's go" until everyone packs up, pays, and leaves. If things go too far before you can get everyone to the extraction point, apologize on the way out, with no trace of a giggle or eye roll whatsoever. *Absolutely none.*

---

* You know, the silent, devastating threat your mom flashes you when you start acting up in front of Grandma.

# YOU CAN HAVE MORE
# THAN ONE RELATIONSHIP
# AT THE SAME TIME!

———

AH, YOUNG LOVE. So all-consuming. So intense. So annoying to everyone around you.

Don't be that asshole who ignores his friends when he starts dating someone. As real as it feels (and, thanks to hormones, it feels pretty freaking real), your young romance may not turn out to be your one and only soul mate. If it doesn't happen to work out, you're going to need to lean on your friends—and it's going to be a lot easier for them to be there for you if you've acknowledged their existence recently.* Fun fact: The love hormone is oxytocin.† You don't want to go through post-breakup withdrawal all alone.

Come up for oxygen once in a while. Your sweetie should understand that you want to spend time with your friends. Make an effort to carve out some time for them. Get together with your friends *and* your significant other's friends. Invite the guys over while Sweetie is off doing something else. Figure it out. The friendships you have now will be the ones you treasure most as a full-fledged grown-up. Why do you think the Olds keep checking Facebook and having those sad, weird high school reunions?

---

\* Sidenote: When you are in love, your family still exists, probably right where you left them.

† Oxytocin is known as the cuddle hormone. OxyContin is a powerfully addictive narcotic that can destroy lives. Given the choice of which one to let into your developing brain, please go with the cuddle one.

## BE A GOOD SPORT

––––

SPORTS ARE THE root of some pretty big misunderstandings about what it means to Act Like a Man. Sports are also the way many guys do friendship, not to mention a great outlet for all those crazy hormones. So you're going to have to learn how to play along.

* *Don't play like your life depends on it.* I know, I know. It's an elimination tournament, or a division championship, or your last chance to break the record. There's always something at stake. That's how sports works. But I promise you, I swear on Cal Ripken Jr.: Many people have come to this same moment before you. Many people have failed. And those people have gone on to lead productive, happy lives. Contrary to what movies have led you to believe, they do not wake up every day for the next forty years, look at their stubbled, pathetic faces in the mirror, and drink beer after beer on brown plaid couches until they pass out so they can avoid thinking about the day they blew the big whatever. You know what they actually do? They keep playing . . . or not. They get on with their lives. They try other things. They get jobs. They make families. They even buy cars and houses, the latter of which are hardly ever decorated with brown plaid couches and piles of empty beer cans.

  What I'm saying is, unless you're an asshole, the camaraderie of sports will outlast the thrill of victory or agony of defeat. People will forget if you made the shot, but they'll remember if you were a showboat or played dirty. They'll also remember if you treated your teammates with respect, gave injured opponents a hand up, helped coaches carry their gear, and took *both* wins *and* losses like a champ. You'll remember who treated you well and who treated you badly—and exactly whom you treated well or badly.

**Assholes throw helmets and storm off.**

**Non-assholes throw the ball.**

**Good guys throw out the Gatorade bottles the rest of the team left behind.**

\* *Engage in the right kind of competition off the field.* In the best kind of competition, everyone plays at the top of his game and to the strengths of each person on the team. This raises the overall level of play, so that, win or lose, everyone is better off for having played. In the worst kind of competition, players focus only on themselves, even if it's damaging to other players and to the game itself.

You know that one asshole who hangs around the edge of your conversations, half listening for the chance to jump in and one-up everybody else? Even when you're talking with him one on one, you can tell it's killing him to "listen," and that he's just biding his time until he can ever so casually mention that his BMI, reps, squats—fill in the blank here—top yours.

Forget that guy. Let him measure his own . . . accomplishments. Friends should bring out the best in each other on and off the field. Be the kind of friend who lifts people up with a little friendly competition, not the asshole who knocks everybody else down.

* *Don't become your own hobby.* Fitness is important. If you feel good, you'll do good. Gym time isn't the only way to be fit, but if that works for you, have at it. There's nothing wrong with getting strong. But I'm going to take a leap here and assume that your personal and professional goals don't require you to perform choreography with your pecs, run a marathon in Death Valley, or drag a tire around with your teeth. Am I right? If this is the case, you probably shouldn't spend more time with your "friends at the gym" than you do with your real friends. If you start believing you need supplements, powders, and gels because normal human food isn't adequate; if you enjoy performing feats of strength only when you have an audience (or—worse!—in front of a mirror); or if you've ever once had a conversation, either with yourself or with any other human being, about the appearance of your veins, you've cruised straight past healthy lifestyle and become one of those assholes whose lifestyle is . . . his own body. Ew.

> **You don't need a gym body or a beach body to go to either of those places— or anywhere else.**

# RULES FOR DRINKING
# WITH BUDDIES

———

ONLY ASSHOLES USE alcohol as an excuse for being assholes. If you're old enough to drink, you're old enough to follow a few basic rules to keep yourself and your friends safe. Don't wait until you're drunk to learn them, either.*

* *Avoid free drugs and alcohol.* Having to pay your own way not only helps you pace yourself but also tends to keep your total intake to non-stomach-pumping levels. Plus, what is your "host" trying to gain by getting you loaded? Exhibit A: Frats let girls drink free but make the boys pay. Don't cosign that.

* *Arrive together. Leave together. Nobody gets left behind.* Do not listen when your drunk friends say, "Go on! I'm fine!" This is an absolutely critical rule. Before you go, make an unbreakable pact not to change the plan after the Fireball kicks in.

* *Don't drink anything some random hands you.* I know that urban legend about waking up in a bathtub of ice with a missing kidney isn't true, but you probably want to hang on to your wallet, too.

* *The thing about shots is that they impair your ability to say no to more shots.* Once you start with the shots, you're not really deciding anything else. Oh, things will happen, but you won't be in control of any of them.

---

* Although I'm sure it would be much more hilarious.

* *Never be the drunkest one in the room.* If you are, you're the asshole everybody has to worry about for the rest of the night.

* *When things go from funny to sad, you are DONE.* You're also done at the precise moment you feel it's imperative to take off your shirt, decide to whip out your cell and start texting a crush, or get an awesome idea that has anything whatsoever to do with live animals. When you start high-fiving asshole talk or behavior, you are over the limit. TIP: Put one person in charge at the beginning of the night to monitor the shenanigans. When it's your turn, make sure everybody in your orbit follows these rules.

* *Do not disgrace yourself or your family.* There's a reason they call it the walk of shame. Actually, the walk of shame is pretty much the best-case scenario. The bathroom floor crawl of shame and the unconscious puke bed of shame are much worse. And clean up after your disgusting self.

* *No tattoos.* Good guys don't let their friends get drunk-tattooed. The goal of any night of drinking should be a good time with **no permanent consequences**. Which brings us to the next few rules . . .

* *If you're old enough to drink, you're old enough to go to real jail.* Hi, I'm your arrest record. When you apply for jobs, people are going to be very interested in me!

* *Make a choice and stick to it.* Decisions about sex require a clear head. If you think too drunk to consent is something like too drunk to walk, you are setting the bar much too low. Instead, remember this: If either one of you is too drunk to walk *through an actual minefield with live ammunition,* there's an excellent chance you're too drunk to navigate consent. The safest bet is to choose between sex and drinking on any given night.

* *Don't drive or get in a car with a driver who is not 100 percent sober.* There is no excuse for this. Only an asshole would even attempt driving after a couple of drinks. Uber or Lyft. Get the car in the morning.

* *Walk this way.* In the moment, you might think it's pretty smart to walk more than a mile home from the party at one a.m. instead of taking your car, but that's the kind of drunk reasoning that gets people killed. If there's any chance you won't be able to stay on course, out of traffic, and out of trouble, walk with a buddy or get an Uber.

* *If you are unsure whether you should call 911, call 911.* Nobody sleeps off dead.

# 3 /

# DON'T
# BE AN
# ASSHOLE
# TO YOUR
# FAMILY

UNLESS YOU ARE A TOTAL IRREDEEMABLE ASSHOLE, I'M guessing you can remember experiencing a terrifying flash of realization at the moment it first occurred to you that one of your parents is an actual living, breathing, mortal human being. Was it that time you saw your dad shed a tear, and it wasn't over a championship game? Or was it when you forgot your mom's birthday and she lost her mind, simultaneously screaming and crying?* Was it that confusing time you caught her quietly weeping on the couch, watching a tribute to some just-dead celebrity you had never even heard of, let alone realized your mom loved in a weirdly intense—dare I say teenagery—way? Your mom! A teenager! With love feelings for someone who makes art!†

Whatever happened, you probably had a squirmy, uncomfortable feeling when the realization struck. Psychologists call this "cognitive dissonance." This happens when you see something with your own eyes that runs contrary to your understanding of the universe. You know your mom as Mom, but then all of a sudden she goes around acting like a person and your brain is confused. Here's

---

* She probably said something like "Just once I would APPRECIATE it if PEOPLE AROUND HERE would think of **SOMEONE BESIDES THEMSELVES**!"— probably.

† RIP, Prince. I will never forget you, my tiny royal purple highness.

the thing: This is happening because you don't treat your mom like a person.

It's not entirely your fault that your parents usually don't seem like people with an actual life.* Many loving parents hide their own feelings about real-life stuff to make sure their kids have as few worries as possible and grow up happy and confident. But there's a difference between validating your feelings and validating asshole behavior. Maybe your family has put up with you until now because they're worried about your self-esteem, too shocked to know how to respond, too tired to fight, or just generally afraid that if they make the wrong move, you'll end up on *Dateline*.

Let's get this cleared up. I understand you have some pretty major fears and frustrations about your daily life, your personal relationships, and YOUR FUTURE. I also know that these feelings can be intense. Their impact looms large, your hormones are raging, and you're still developing the skills to cope with what's going on inside your head. But if you think any of this entitles you to shit all over your family, you are an asshole.

---

* Real talk: If you know full well that your parents are human because they have let you down—not in a forgot-to-sign-the-permission-slip way but in a serious thing-that-shouldn't-happen-to-a-kid, heart-changing way, I am very, very sorry. You deserve better.

# YOUR PARENTS ARE NOT YOUR EMPLOYEES

———

Do NOT TELL your parents what to do. *Ask* them. Nicely, like your next move actually depends on the answer, not while you're already doing the thing you're "asking" about. If the answer is no, do *not* throw a mantrum.* Red-faced shouting, door slamming, and foot stomping will not convince your parents that you are mature enough to do the thing you want.

| JERK THING TO SAY | BETTER THING TO SAY |
| --- | --- |
| I'm taking the car. | May I use the car to go to play practice [that will occur several hours—or even days—from now]? |
| | TIP: Try not to have the keys in your hand when you ask. |
| *At 6:00 a.m. or 10:00 p.m.:* I need a [calculator, band shirt, poster board] for school by today. | Would you please help me get the [whatever] my teacher requires? I'm supposed to have it by next week or [say what will happen if you don't have it by then]. |
| | TIP: Your teacher is the boss of you, not the boss of your parents. You still have to ask. Ahead of time.† |

TABLE 2: *How to Get What You Want from Your Parents*

———

* A "mantrum" is the exact same thing as a toddler-style tantrum except that it is thrown by someone whose voice has changed and/or who is over five feet tall. In other words, it is *not* cute.

† In this case, "ahead of time" means while Amazon Prime is still a possibility. Your parents are not huge fans of rearranging their whole day to deal with your "emergency." Nor do they love changing out of their sweatpants and heading back out after you "just remembered" you "need" something.

| JERK THING TO SAY | BETTER THING TO SAY |
| --- | --- |
| I'm going out with my friends. | Would it be OK if I meet up with the guys at Wingstop and then go to Jake's house [again, at a specific time in the future]?<br><br>TIP: Throw in a couple of details about what you're doing so that your parent has some information upon which to base a decision. If there's no *decision* involved, you're not technically *asking*. |
| I need new clothes. | Could we go shopping this weekend? I was thinking about getting some new shoes [but I can wait if time or budget does not allow].<br><br>TIP: Non-assholes know the difference between "want" and "need," and understand that, even though time and money are imaginary constructs, they have actual limits in the real world. |
| There's nothing to eat. | I finished the [milk, bread, cereal, granola bars, peanut butter, dozen apples—whatever you just tossed down your gaping maw]. Could you please stop at the store on your way home?<br><br>TIP: This request will be much better received if you actually make it, by text or call, before the parent in question is, in fact, inside your home. |
| The guys are coming over. | Would it be OK if the guys came over [at a specific time in the future] to [specify what you will be doing] in [specify what room needs cleaning]? Could we please have some [indicate what mass quantities of food are expected]?<br><br>Bonus points: Indicate how many guys are coming and when they are leaving. |

TABLE 2: *How to Get What You Want from Your Parents (continued)*

# DON'T TAKE EVERYTHING OUT ON THE FAM

——

You HAD A bad day. Don't be an asshole and take it out on the people who love you. They are also humans, as shocking as that seems right now.

Here's another fancy psychology term for you: *object permanence.* It's the stage when a baby realizes that a block under a blanket is still a block. You've got that one down, but have you figured out that your human family still exists when you're not with them? I promise you, the fam abides. While you were at school, your parents had a day, too. They may well have spent it performing thankless tasks aimed at making your life better. They do not deserve garbage treatment because your coach or true love or whoever did you wrong.

Thought experiment: Next time Dad asks you what happened today, instead of saying "Nothing," why don't you tell him about the jerk third-period teacher who locks you out every time your even worse second-period teacher keeps you late? You can blow off a little steam, maybe get a little sympathy, possibly even come up with a plan. Then, instead of irrationally blowing up at whoever's responsible for the empty fridge (you, by the way) or your dirty uniform (also you), you can simmer down and act like a normal person.

Now, your dad may not offer any sympathy. I'm sorry about that. I truly am. I don't know why so many dads are like this. Maybe it's because their dads were the same way and they got stuck with some terribly old-fashioned idea of what it means to Be a Man.* You'll need to find another way to navigate your feelings

---

* Dads have feelings, I promise. Moms know these things. If you take my advice and share what's going on instead of following their stoic example, maybe we can help the dads out and show them a better way than pretending nothing affects them and going berserk every time someone cuts them off in traffic.

and avoid mistreating the family (yes, including him). If you don't have a friend or ally, you need to cultivate one. One person you can reach out to using whatever technology is comfortable for you. That sounds doable, right?*

No? OK, then you're going to have to find another way. Maybe it's a workout, a song, a podcast, a nap—a safe and ready way to downshift your brain into a lower gear, where you can handle things that don't go your way at a non-asshole rpm. Don't go with drinking, drugs, smoking, or vaping. These things are addictive and can slowly kill you, so it may not be the best idea to intentionally wire your brain to need them to get through the day.

If you need a little time to cool off before facing your family, go ahead and say so. But here's a hint: It really helps if you can keep the tone of your man voice as rage-free as possible. Tone is really important. What you're going for is a calm, quiet, and even voice—much more Bob Ross† than Bobby Knight.‡ Compare:

**I need, like, A HALF HOUR to think! Can't we put this on hold FOR, LIKE, 30 MINUTES?!**

**I need, like, a half hour to think. Can we please put this on hold for, like, 30 minutes?**

---

* Be a good guy and think about being this person for someone else while you're at it.

† Bob Ross is a real person who had a PBS television show so far before your time that now he's retro-cool. He would make a painting while talking about/to the painting in a peaceful and quiet voice. That's it. That's the whole show. I'm not even kidding. YouTube it.

‡ Bobby Knight was once the chair-throwing coach of the Indiana University men's basketball team, legendary for either winning games or throwing epic mantrums, depending on whether the person describing him is an asshole. YouTube it. Then never ever do anything you see.

## TREAT YOUR RELATIVES BETTER

ONCE UPON A time, when someone on the playground uttered a swear word, the standard retort was "You kiss your mother with that mouth?" The implication was that the potty mouth naturally respected his mother *more* than anyone else and ought to extend some of that same respect to his classmates. Believe it or not, foul-mouthed bullies were actually chagrined by this.

### *ASSHOLE DEAD GIVEAWAY*

*Eye rolls his momma in Target,
where all the other moms are
**definitely** watching.*

Nothing gets my side-eye going quite like hearing someone your age talking to his mom in a disrespectful tone that I know for absolute sure he would never take with his coach, his teacher, any of his friends, or even a complete stranger. How is it OK to snap at the person who dedicates her life to your health and happiness but then offer a cheery "No problem!" to the slacker cashier who takes three tries to ring you up? It's quite the mystery. Know this: If you keep talking to your mother like she's dog poop in the treads of the Jordans *that she bought you*, you will eventually face the consequences.*

**An asshole treats his family worse than he treats complete strangers.**

**A non-asshole keeps it civil.**

**A good guy gives his family:**

* *the same benefit of the doubt he gives a stranger,*
* *the same respect he gives a coach,*
* *the same patience he gives his most clueless friend, and*
* *the same kindness he extends to his amigos.*

---

\* If any moms are reading this, please feel free to loudly remind your disrespectful son exactly where he came from, loudly using the word "vagina" in Target or wherever you happen to be. I will fully support you by nodding and raising a silent universal sign of peace, the V.

# SORRY:
# THERE ARE NO MAGIC WORDS

———

THE OLDS MAY have given toddler-you the wrong idea by insisting you "saaaay the ma-gic wur-huuurrrd!" I hate to break the spell, but there are no magic words. What you *say* doesn't matter as much as what you *do*.

Even though a front-facing camera takes them by surprise every single time, your parents are no dummies. They know that when you add a dramatic or ingratiating "please!" at the end of your entitled demand, you're not really asking permission. They can also tell when you grumble a reluctant "thanks" that, rather than feeling the slightest pang of appreciation, you resent having to ask at all.

But the worst—for both them and for you—the absolute worst, is that they instantly know from how thoughtlessly you say "sorry" that you don't mean it, not even a little. To avoid being an asshole, you need to learn how to apologize for real.

**1.** *Know what you are apologizing for.* What did you do wrong? Answering this question is not fun, because you have to examine your behavior and determine where it was lacking. Do it anyway. Think about it (with your brain, please, and preferably for more than one minute). If you don't figure out where you went wrong, you'll never learn.

If you honestly don't know what you did wrong (after you think about it, with your brain, for more than one minute), ask. Not in a passive-aggressive "OBviously you think I'm TERRible and can't do ANYthing right. WHAT is it this time?" kind of way, but in a "Hey, I feel like I owe you an apology but I'm confused about what happened. Can we talk about it?" good-guy kind of way. And here's the real trick: Listen to the answer. The whole thing. Hear the person out without throwing a mantrum. Don't jump out with explanations and excuses. Let the person finish talking. Try to imagine the situation from his or her point of view. Then acknowledge the person and buy yourself some time for proper brain thinking by saying, "Thanks for telling me. I'll think about what you said."

2. *Know to whom you owe the apology.* This calls for some AP-level analysis, because—you may want to take a note here in case it's on the exam—*it may be more than one person.* Royal screwups tend to disappoint multiple people. Who did you let down? Your friends? Your classmates? Your parents? Think about it (with your brain for more than one minute). If anyone's giving you the cold shoulder, sighing, or looking at the floor, shaking their head when you walk by, consider it a major clue.

3. *Accept responsibility for your actions.* To make a proper apology, you need to say what you did, starting with the word "I." You don't have to perform a soliloquy, but you do need to say enough words that the other person knows *that you know* exactly what you did wrong.

> TERRIBLE: *I'm sorry that you got upset.*

> BETTER: *I'm sorry that I said your new haircut makes you look like Dwight Schrute. I suck.*

4. *Do not make your apology conditional.* Only assholes issue conditional apologies. If you include the word "if" or "but" in your so-called apology, you are an asshole and a weasel.*

---

* And maybe you should think about becoming a politician.

THE WORST: *I'm sorry if you took it the wrong way.*

BETTER: *I'm sorry **that** I said you're a complete moron. Maybe the Lions will surprise us this year.*

5. *Choose the right time and place.* DO NOT APOLOGIZE BY TEXT. The sound of your apology needs to come out of your mouth hole and go directly into the other person's ear hole, preferably while you are looking them right in the eye holes. No texting, and absolutely no vague social media mea culpa—that's nonsense. Man up and do it. Call if you have to, but apologize in person when you can.

6. *That thing that hurts people? Don't do it again.* This is the number one most important thing about apologies. The "I learned my lesson" part. The "I won't do it again" part. If you *say* you're sorry but then you turn around and do it again, everybody knows from that moment on that your apology means nothing. Your family's love is unconditional, but their trust is not. You might think it's no big deal when the apology is for a small thing like forgetting to bring in the trash cans, but the fact that you need to apologize at all is a major tip-off that it's only a small thing *to you*. Go back to #1.

*Parental-blood-pressure-reducing bonus tip:* Your parents would rather not spend their time lecturing you over and over on basic expectations of living. They don't wake up in the morning hoping you leave your clothes on the floor so they can launch into their very favorite command performance of "Who do you think cleans up around here?" You can wow them with your maturity and growth by doing actual mindful things like putting clothes in the hamper, not leaving dishes in the sink, and putting the seat down in the bathroom. Do these things and save your apologies for the big stuff.

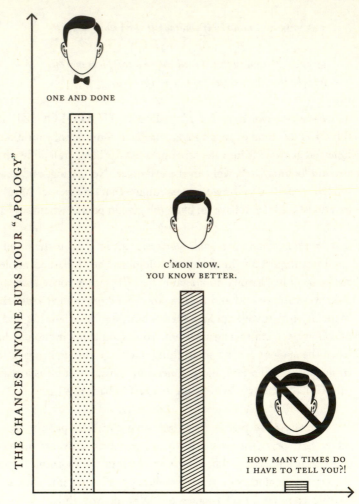

THE CHANCES ANYONE BUYS YOUR "APOLOGY"

ONE AND DONE

C'MON NOW.
YOU KNOW BETTER.

HOW MANY TIMES DO
I HAVE TO TELL YOU?!

NUMBER OF TIMES YOU DO THE THING

FIGURE 4: *The Limits of Apology*

## YOU CAN COME HOME AGAIN
## (JUST DON'T EFF IT UP)

———

HAVE YOU BEEN away from home for more than a sleepover? Summer camp? College? Juvie? If you've left, experienced some new things, and come back evolved as a person, that's great. And if you haven't yet, don't worry. Soon enough, the time will come for you to strike out on your own. And you will.*

Wherever you are in this process, there's something you need to know. Only assholes think that temporarily leaving home or turning eighteen auto-magically means that they no longer answer to anyone and now get to do whatever they want.

First of all, becoming an adult is a process. Use this checklist of typical adulting tasks to determine how close you are to becoming a member of the A-Team:

⊘ Do you cook for yourself? With food that you bought? With your own money?

⊘ Do you clean up after yourself? Like, as a regular thing, not only when someone is threatening to throw your stuff out into the street?

⊘ Do you do your own laundry? Before it gets crunchy?

⊘ Do you have two sheets on your bed and two curtains in your shower?†

———

* You will, right? RIGHT?! Of course you will.

† Yes, two shower curtains. One is a liner. Go to Bed Bath & Beyond and get one.

◎ Do you pay for your housing? With money? That you made? Legally?

◎ Do you pay for your transportation? Not just the gas but the car payment and insurance, too? Is the Uber/Lyft account tied to your very own credit card, not a parent's?

◎ Do you pay for your own cell phone plan? No one is interested in your argument about how keeping you on the family plan makes it cheaper. A simple yes or no will do, please.

◎ Do you know how to bank? And post office? Make your own doctor appointments and not hang up in a panic when they ask for your insurance information?

◎ Do you ever watch PBS?* On purpose?

Unless you answered yes to all these questions, you are not yet an adult. Anytime you're wondering why your parents aren't treating you like an adult, have a look at this list and maybe try to check off an item or two. Voluntarily. By the way, it's OK to ask about all these things!

Your growing up is a process for your parents, too. Even though the writing was on the wall from the very first moment you existed, they just cannot believe it's happening—maybe due to some kind of Darwinian blind spot that's tricked them into still seeing you as a helpless little baby so they continue caring for you instead of kick-

---

* PBS is a television network that old people watch. On an actual television-sized television.

ing your ass out. Stop *telling* them that you're an adult and start to *show* them.

### KEEP IT SWEET: HOW TO COME HOME

* *When you come home, don't call it a visit.* Trust me, it's like a knife in the heart. Just say you're coming home. We all love the sound of that.

* *You're not the King of the World.* People may be glad to see you. They may want to spoil you. Enjoy it, but don't act like you deserve it. If you want to come home a conquering hero, pitch in. Do your own wash and act like it's no big deal. Give the younger sibs you left behind a break and clear the table.* Help someone without being asked. It will blow all their minds.

* *Ask us about our lives.* Remember, when you are away, the family abides. You can demonstrate mastery of this adult-level concept by asking everyone what happened while you were gone, thus proving that your developing mind is capable of recognizing your family's continued existence when they are not with you. TIP: Listen to what your family says and ask them to say more about it. Don't immediately jump to your thing, which signals you don't really give a crap.

---

* In case you haven't realized it yet, when you get older you're going to really appreciate your siblings, so maybe don't be an asshole to them, even if they're younger and still assholes themselves. Trust me on this: Nobody will *ever* laugh harder at your impressions of Mom and Dad.

* *Don't assume you are the smartest person in the room.* Your parents will be thrilled to learn that they're getting their money's worth with that college tuition, but there's no way that, in just fifteen weeks, you became the only person on earth who knows anything about anything. You learned stuff. Congrats. Don't be an asshole about it. Just because you really understand statistics now doesn't mean you should ruin the rest of our Powerball dreams. (*See also:* You took one film class and now we can never watch a movie with you again.)

* *Things haven't changed. They've just changed for you.* Did you have a curfew before you left? Did you have to ask before you used the car? Were you expected home for dinner? Just because the rules away from home are different doesn't mean the house rules have changed. If you think a house rule change is in order, ask. Calmly. Like an adult next in line at the post office sweetly trying to persuade the clerk to help just one more customer before shutting down for his lunch break.* And if your parents don't give you the answer you want, avoid throwing a mantrum. Maybe they'll be impressed with your mature reaction and keep thinking about it.

* *Promptly answer calls and texts from the people who love you enough to keep you on the family mobile phone plan.* Do it before they lose their minds and start thinking about calling around to hospitals and police stations, which is usually in about one hour. Parents have active imaginations from watching too

---

* I'm telling you, post office skills are key.

much *CSI,* so get back to them quickly with proof of life and
spare yourself the drama.*

* *Good guys come bearing gifts.* Sure, you could do an emergency
detour into a highway rest stop or the college bookstore and
buy everybody the same exact Koozie, but the best gifts show
that you know an individual person in a real way by showing
that you *understand*—what they enjoy, or what they hope, or
who they are. You know your family better than you know
anyone. Give it some thought, and more time than money.
You got this.

* *Keep it PG-13.* Do you like picturing your parents having
sex? What a surprise. They don't want to picture you
doing it either. Your parents are not ready to deal with your
sexcapades—or your hangovers, for that matter, so don't start
helping yourself to their beer. Oh, and they know what weed
smells like, even if you try to blow it out the window. You're
not home long. Deal with it.

---

* When your parents' "call" is shouted down the stairs in the general direction of
your gaming lair, say "Yes?" instead of "WHAT!"—which sounds totally angry and
rude in your man voice. Be careful with that man voice!

# 4

# DON'T
# BE AN
# ASSHOLE
# AT
# WORK

SSUMING YOU'RE ON BOARD WITH THE WHOLE GET-money, move-out, have-a-life plan, you're going to need a job. You may have gotten the wrong idea about work from inspirational Instagram quotes like "Do what you love and you'll never work a day in your life." You may also have become confused by the number of people (usually the ones worried about your college applications) telling you that you need to "find your passion."

Reality check: Most people work to get money. If you're lucky, you'll end up in a job that pays you enough money to offset its negatives. I'm sorry to break it to you, but that job is probably a long way off for you. For now, the most important job skill you can possess is the ability to do things that seem boring and useless without acting like an asshole.

Think back on your most glorious memory. Maybe it was that big game when you made that incredible sports ball play and got all the points. (Fill in your own memory here.) Wow. That was amazing! But you have to admit that getting there was hard work. You collapsed and puked on the sports place a hundred times in practice, but when the moment arrived, your dedication paid off. You enjoyed a true sense of accomplishment, the appreciation of your peers, and (most probably) a nice, shiny trophy.

I hate to be the one to tell you this, but at work you don't get the trophy. You do all the running and the puking and somebody else victoriously crosses the finish line and accepts the medal "for the team." That's just how work works. It sucks sometimes, but you don't get to be an asshole about it, because if you are, they stop giving you money. This is what the Olds call "paying your dues."

If "entry level" isn't exactly goals for you, you need to start thinking about how to level up. Now. Yes, even if you don't have a job yet. The two-step trick of making it through every shitty job and moving on to a better one is to:

1. Make sure the job gets you a little closer to a job you actually want.

2. Take good advantage of every opportunity you're given.

# WHAT DO YOU
# WANT TO DO?

———

**IF YOU KNOW** what you want to do, you can start plotting a course to get there. This is why the Olds keep telling you to "find your passion." Seems sensible, right?

But how are you supposed to know what your passion is when you're trapped in school all day and not allowed to do anything you want? Good news: The part of your life where you get to try new things and decide if you like them is still ahead of you. Stop worrying about finding your "true passion" and just think about this:

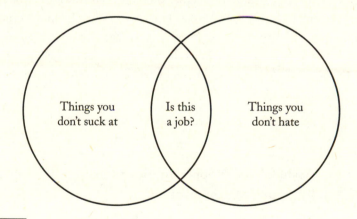

FIGURE 5: *Passion Schmassion, or How to Find a Job*

If this is your first job, you may only have enough information to come up with a couple of pretty general ideas for these two categories, like "computers" or "music." That's OK. The more general you are, the easier it is to find a job where you can learn a little bit about that thing. If you don't suck at games and don't hate being outside, awesome! Camp counselor is a job. If you get a camp counselor job and you love it, good! You know you're on the right track. If you hate it, good! Now you know what to cross off the list next time.

Even if you hate the job—*especially* if you hate the job—you can't be an asshole at work. First of all, they're paying you money not to be an asshole. Second of all, if you get fired or piss people off, you're going to miss out on the Golden Ticket to your next better job: the recommendation. Your boss and your coworkers may think of you when they hear about a new opportunity, or not. They may let you know about it, or not. They could even recommend you, or not. Don't wait until you need a reference to consider whether your boss and coworkers would recommend you: Are you on time? Do you work hard? How do you take criticism? Do you cooperate with other team members? Do you finish what you start? The Olds call this your reputation, but people these days call it your personal brand. Don't let your brand be asshole.

**Assholes waste opportunities to get ahead by getting fired or quitting.**

**Non-assholes show up, do what's expected, and leave with a decent recommendation.**

**Love it or hate it, good guys work hard enough to be missed when they go, building a network of supporters.**

# A LITTLE MONEY GOES . . .
# WELL . . . A LITTLE WAY

THERE'S ANOTHER PRETTY terrible truth that you need to know at the outset of this whole working business: Generally speaking, when you're first starting out, the less attractive a job is, the less you get paid. I know this makes no sense, but I'm not in charge. Do not expect your starting wage to provide the same life your parents gave you. Your parents worked hard. For a long, long time. They are probably too traumatized at the memory to tell you how little money they had when they first started working. If they did, you might never move out. But they also probably never mentioned how special it was when they saved up over a few paychecks and treated themselves to a crappy meal out. If you manage your money carefully and work hard, you, too, can truly enjoy shitty restaurants!

One other thing—sorry, I know this is a lot of bad news: Your hourly wage multiplied by the number of hours you work does NOT equal the money you get. Taxes (federal, state, *and* local), your share of any benefits your employer offers,* and lots of other weird stuff you never thought about all get deducted before the money lands in your account. Don't start spending before that first payday, because that's when you'll find out how much you're actually getting paid. Grown-ass working people call this "net" or "take-home" pay.

By this point it should be starting to dawn on you that the goal of every terrible-paying job is to move up to a less terrible-paying job ASAP. Now you're ready to learn how to work.

---

* "Benefits" sounds like your employer pays for it, but often the cost is split. Tricky!

## LEARN THE BASICS: HOW TO WORK

——

IN EVERY NEW job, the first order of business is figuring out how to be valuable. Your first big clue will be understanding what they hired you to do. But there's more to this mystery. What tasks are left undone because other people hate doing them? Do those. What makes the boss happy? Do more of that. What makes the boss grumpy? Do less of that. Who does everybody side-eye? Don't be like that person. Who does everybody love? Be more like that person. If all of this sounds kind of abstract, it's because your value really depends on the specific situation and mix of people at your particular job. But there are some universal ways to stay out of asshole territory and become the MVP.

* *Get enough sleep to show up on time and do good work. Every day.* Sure, work time is work time and your time is your time, but if you show up at work unshowered and hungover from a night drinking, gaming, or sexing, you're an asshole. Your boss is paying you to *do the job,* not just to grace the workplace with your physical presence. If you have the kind of job where people's safety depends on you being alert, you better show up rested and ready. If you have the kind of job where you don't think anyone notices whether you get through, say, six inches of paperwork or twelve—you're wrong. People notice.*

* *Be accountable.* It's pretty simple, really. Do what you're supposed to do, when you're supposed to do it. Even if it turns out to be harder or more complicated than you expected, find a

---

* If you ever, ever close your eyes at work "for a sec," you are not earning your keep. Also, everyone saw you and will be talking about it for the rest of the week. Or forever.

way to get your shit done. Some of the shit you have to do will be terrible. Do it anyway. Sometimes, maybe most of the time, you won't feel like doing it. Remind yourself: This shit is why I have a job. This is what the money's for. Then do it. Nothing is worthless if somebody's willing to pay you for it.

If your boss and your coworkers come to count on you to get shit done, you'll generally be able to keep a job. If you do *more* than you're supposed to do, and you manage to do it *faster* than you're supposed to do it, you're on your way to a *better* job. Your boss may give you other, less terrible shit to do. At the least, he'll have no choice but to give you a Golden Ticket recommendation when you find something better. Either way, it's hard to keep a good guy down.

* *Ask for help.* It can be terrifying to tell your boss that you need something explained, especially if you were already shown how to do it and still can't get it to work right. But here's the thing: The unavoidable consequences of faking it totally outweigh the momentary embarrassment of asking for help. People who only *pretend* they know what they're doing can screw things up in incredible ways. Don't be that asshole. Ask if you don't know.

* *Be careful with the tech.* You may know for a fact that you can stock shelves or plate salads or enter data faster when you're motivated by your perfect playlist, but what really matters is *what your boss thinks* every time she has to wait for you to rip out your earbuds.* Along those same lines, you may be 100 percent

---

* Option 1: Look at him go! He is *in the zone.* Option 2: Why am I paying him to listen to podcasts while I stand here waiting?

capable of sending a few texts while sitting in on a meeting, but somebody invited you into the room for a reason.* You may think you're the first truly gifted multitasker your workplace has ever seen, but trust me, you're not. If no one else has three screens fired up and noise-canceling headphones on, there may be a good reason. Could it be that somebody up the line— someone who approves the time sheets, perhaps—equates focus to discipline? Or maybe it's fine. Don't assume. Ask.

## EMAIL: AN INEFFICIENT BUT ANCIENT WORKPLACE TRADITION

⊘ Read every email. Yes, the whole entire thing. I know! So many words!

⊘ If the email is directed to you personally, answer it. Replying "Got it!" or "Will do!" means you got it and are taking care of it. No reply means . . . who knows? Did you get it? Did you get it but not read it? Did you read it and ignore it? Keeping people guessing is not a good strategy.

⊘ Be a copycat until you figure out what's what. If someone emails you using the Olds' English, you should reply in complete sentences. If people start their emails with "Hello!" say "Hello!" back when replying or you might seem like an asshole. VERY IMPORTANT EXCEPTION: Do not participate in any endless one-upping thank-you contest or jump on the Reply All bandwagon.†

---

\* Just guessing here, but that reason is *probably* not so they can watch you texting.

† If you *ever* hit REPLY ALL on an all-staff email, I am coming for you.

❋ *You are not at work to make friends.* You might make friends at work. In fact, you probably will. Working with people you like is great. It makes it easier to get up and get going in the morning. It makes the workday more enjoyable. It might even help you get shit done. But making friends is not the *reason* you go to work. Making money is the reason you go to work. So if the social consequences of your work decisions become more important to you than the work consequences of your work decisions, you've got problems. If you've got problems, your boss has problems. Don't make problems.

For example, do you find yourself mostly agreeing with the work ideas of people you feel comfortable around personally? Do you only have the backs of people whom you like? Or who like you? Which colleagues are in your group chat? Who are you texting? Do those people happen to be your same age? And race? And gender? Don't be the victim of your own unconscious bias. Think about who should be included. Think about *why* you like an idea or don't like an idea. And remember: Business is business.

❋ *Learn to (not) speak the language.* Work is kind of like a scene from a Mafia movie, where a few gentlemen are standing around, all normal-like, and one of them says, ever so casually, "I think we may have a little problem with Paulie." The individuals present understand immediately that "may have a little problem" means "definitely have a big major problem." One of them nods and quietly offers, "I'll take care of it." This obviously means Paulie is about to get whacked. Work is sort of like this—not with the whacking but with the unspoken subtext. Work conversation is *all* about the subtext.

When you're at work, you don't need to convey the degree
of your frustration, because everybody else works there, too.
They already know your pain. Instead, you need to translate
the screaming inside your head into a calm, workplace-friendly
communication before you open your mouth. If it helps,
imagine you're wearing a wire and your boss is listening in.

* *Accept that most of the time, you don't get to decide.* Even if your
  idea is brilliant and you offer it in the most non-judgmental,
  collaborative way possible, you may get shut down. You're not
  the boss. The boss is the boss. Suck it up, keep taking the
  money, and try again next time. Never throw a mantrum at
  work. But you knew that, right?

| DO NOT BLURT THIS AT WORK | TRY THIS INSTEAD, AND USE YOUR MOST SINCERE INSIDE VOICE |
| --- | --- |
| What an effing waste of time! | What will this be used for? |
| I have *NO CLUE* what you're talking about. | Could I have more background before I start? |
| Have you morons **even heard of XYZ?!** | Have you thought about trying XYZ? |
| What IDIOT decided to do it like this? | Can I make a suggestion that might save some time? |
| You don't know what you're talking about. | Not sure I follow. Could you take me through it step by step? |
| WRONG! This is so, so wrong. | I have a slightly different take. |

TABLE 3: *Workplace Translator, or How to Speak Subtext*

## OTHER PEOPLE ARE ALSO AT WORK

——

**YOUR FIRST JOB** may be your first close encounter with someone different from you. Your coworkers may be older, from a different culture, or even women. They are there for the same reason you are: to do work. Don't assume an older person is completely useless about tech, don't ask someone who doesn't look exactly like you where they are from, and scrub from your brain any idea that women are at work to get compliments from you about their bodies.

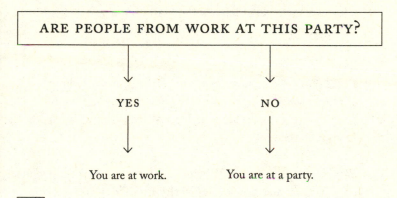

FIGURE 6: *How to Never Embarrass Yourself or Ruin Your Career at Office Parties*

## ALL YOU REALLY NEED TO KNOW ABOUT WORK YOU LEARNED IN PRESCHOOL

———

NERVOUS ABOUT YOUR first day at your first job? Don't be. You learned how to play well with others way back in preschool and it should come a lot easier to you now (assuming you don't get too hungry or tired).

* *Take what you get and don't get upset.* Some days you're the line leader and some days you're the caboose. Take whatever job you're assigned and make the most of it. Don't be the kid crying at the end of the line. Be the greatest caboose who ever caboosed.

* *Be ready to kill it at circle time.* That kid who never brought anything for show-and-tell? Now he's the guy walking into every meeting unprepared, saying, "What is this about again?" Do not be that guy.

* *Skip the wet paper towel.* When you fall down,* be the kid who pops back up and keeps going with dirt all over his face, not the kid who needs the teacher to coo over him with a wet paper towel. We're working here. Nobody has time to go get you a wet paper towel.

---

* By the way, if you never fall down, you're not playing hard enough.

* *Rise above the paste eaters.* Did you finish cutting out and gluing your thing together while the people around you were still eating paste? Don't just sit there waiting for them to catch up or, worse, start eating the paste, too. Raise your hand and ask what you can do next.

* *Don't blame your imaginary friend.* Did you spill juice everywhere? Did you (whispers) have an accident? Don't blame it on your imaginary friend or make up some big story about how it wasn't your fault. Everybody knows what's up. You blew it. Just say you blew it, apologize, and help clean up.

* *It's not always your turn to shine.* Other people get to be Star of the Week or VIP, too. When it's someone else's time to shine, throw a little light their way instead of grumbling in a corner that it should have been you: "Great job on that presentation, Angela! Your slides were really effective!"*

* *Manners matter.* Just like in preschool, at work we say please and thank you. At the end of the day,† think about who made it possible for you to get your shit done. Thank that person, with words you form with your mouth, while looking into their eyes, in the vicinity of their ears: "Thanks for helping me with that report today, Toby!"

---

* Don't expect your boss to praise you the way your preschool teacher did. Good job, by the way!

† "At the end of the day" is something people say at work to mean "I don't really care about all that other stuff we just talked about. We're doing what I'm about to say." But in this case it literally means at the end of your workday, when you leave work.

## STEER CLEAR OF ASSHOLES

ONE OF THE best and worst things about work is that there are other people there. *Best* because other people will help you get your bearings, mentor and encourage you, and contribute to your success.

*Worst* because some of those other people are assholes.

## *ASSHOLE DEAD GIVEAWAY*

### *Always takes the credit and spreads the blame.*

Depending on the size of your workplace and the makeup of your immediate team, assholes can be an occasional annoyance, or they can make life downright miserable. The question you ultimately have to ask yourself is: Am I getting paid enough to deal with this asshole?—not on any particular day, but over the course of the job. If the answer is yes, if the pros outweigh the cons and you want to stay, you'll have to find a way to deal. You can talk to HR, try to ignore the asshole, find a way to empathize, laugh it off, or avoid the person. But *whatever* you do, don't fight asshole with asshole. Once you give off even the teeny-tiniest whiff of asshole, it's highly unlikely you'll come out smelling like a rose.

If the answer is no—if you're dealing with an abusive or toxic person on a regular basis and it's affecting your life outside of work— you need to consider leaving.

## HOW AND WHEN TO LEAVE

———

IF YOU MAKE a habit of quitting, you're going to have a hard time getting ahead. At each job, it takes time to gain the combination of experience and trust that can lead to new opportunities. It's also a challenge to get any kind of recommendation when you didn't stick around long enough to do what you said you were going to do. Before you quit, think about why you took the job—how you thought it would help you up the ladder—and be honest with yourself about whether you've given it enough time to get what you wanted. Did you learn everything there is to learn? Have you met everyone there is to meet? Is there nothing new here for you to do? OK, then maybe it's time to plan your next move.

If not, how bad is it? Maybe you had a bad day at work. Maybe you had a bad week. Maybe you even had a bad month. None of these is the same thing as having a bad *job*. Ask yourself, Are they paying me enough to put up with this shit? Think about the whole picture—the money, the time, busy and slow seasons, the mix of people who come and go, what other work is out there.

You also need to take your personal financial situation into account, especially if you don't have another gig lined up. Plenty of people put up with a crap ton of shit just to make their student loan payments. The faster you pay them off, the more flexibility you'll have later on when your greater work experience gives you more opportunities to consider. And think twice about going without health insurance. It would be nice if you weren't bankrupted by a single unexpected emergency room visit, wouldn't it?

Don't get me wrong. There are some jobs that are not worth it. Some bosses will take advantage of young or inexperienced people, asking them to do work that's unsafe, that's illegal, or that just wasn't part of the bargain. You might get cheated on hours or wages. The working environment might be manipulative or abusive. *None of this is OK.* In this scenario, go ahead and walk out. And let somebody in authority know what's going on to reduce the chances that this bullshit will continue.

Otherwise, for your regular, run-of-the-mill, I'm-just-so-done-with-this type of job exit, it's a **very, very bad idea** to burn bridges. If the job you're leaving has anything at all to do with your long-term interests, it's likely that you're going to come across some of the same people again. Why do you think the Olds are always running into people they know and saying "What are the chances?!" It's because the chances are good.

## HOW TO LEAVE A JOB AND STAY GOLDEN

⊘ Give reasonable notice so the team is prepared to take on your work.

⊘ Provide a calm, rational, profanity-free reason for leaving. People your age usually say something like "I really enjoyed working here. It's just time to explore other opportunities."*

⊘ Thank your soon-to-be-old boss for the opportunity—and you are thankful, because you made the most of it, right?

⊘ Don't talk crap about anything or anybody on the way out.

---

* This is one of those Mafia situations I was talking about. Everybody knows this means you're over it. You don't have to say you're over it. Trust me.

⊘ Don't brag about your next job.

⊘ Don't steal or wreck anything. Not even a little.

⊘ Exchange contact info, not only with buddies and potential dates, but with anyone who might be kind enough to give you advice down the road.*

⊘ GET THE GOLDEN TICKET. Shake hands, look people in the eyes, and say, "Could I reach out to you for a recommendation in the future?"

---

* LinkedIn is great for this, because work people only post work stuff there, which means there's almost no chance of anybody seeing something . . . let's say, unhelpful to your career.

# 5

# DON'T
# BE AN
# ASSHOLE
# ON THE
# MOVE

YOU ARE GOING PLACES! YOU'VE EARNED SOME INDEPEN-
dence and maybe a little money, and you're starting to strike
out on your own instead of riding shotgun in the minivan.
That's great! Maybe you're walking to the public bus, getting on the
subway, driving a car, or calling an Uber. However you're getting
around, there's a whole entire world of people out there for you to
piss off!

Oops. Apparently when young men begin to escape their parents' clutches and gain a little independence, they lose their minds.
I'm not exactly sure why this happens, so you tell me. Is it because
you think when your parents can't see you it doesn't matter what you
do? Are you testing the limits of your newfound freedom? Do you
think you're invincible? Do you just not know the ropes? What is
going on here?

Here's the thing: When you are in the company of your parents and you act like an asshole, people will place the blame partly
on your parents for not doing their job. When you keep your own
company and act like an asshole, it's *all you*. Plus, you look like a
man and sound like a man and you're doing man things now, so
the people you piss off are going to respond as if you're a man—
not a dumb kid who doesn't know any better and deserves a break.
So, although you may be under the impression that you're *less*

accountable after you give your keepers the slip, you're actually *more* accountable.*

Why should you care if strangers think you're an asshole? Because strangers are just humans you don't know yet. *The whole world is strangers.* Strangers can show you the way or they can steer you wrong. They can make room for you or they can box you out. They can give you a helping hand or they can decide to call the cops. It is human nature to give the good guy a break.†

## *The kindness of strangers is real.*

If you have never experienced it, that may be because you are acting like it's your first time outside, and the people around you would like you to go back inside and stay there.

---

* Sorry to break it to you. I know, it's disappointing.

† Oh, and being a good guy makes the world a better place.

# WALK THIS WAY

———

I **KNOW SOMEONE** taught you pedestrian safety rules when you were little, but that was before you started rebelling against authority and thinking you're too smart and/or invincible to worry about little things like pedestrian safety rules. It was also before you got a phone that's more fascinating to you than life, even if real life is coming toward you at 50 miles per hour while also looking at its own fascinating phone. So here's a little refresher:

* *Cross at the intersection.* Yes, I know you're tall and smart and fast and can get across four lanes and a median on the diagonal in plenty of time. Cross at the crosswalk anyway. It's where drivers are expecting to encounter you. Drivers include people on their phones, people who forgot their glasses, people racing to the hospital with a sick kid—you name it. You can't count on them to keep you safe, especially when you surprise them. Count on yourself.*

* *If there's a light, wait for the light.* Even if no one's in sight and it's taking forever? That's the same thing the asshole in the fast-approaching Mustang is thinking, so stay put. Go ahead and push that little traffic signal button a hundred times if it helps you endure the wait.

* *Look both ways, then don't look at your phone until you get to the other side.* Yes, I know. It's very far. It might be one whole

---

* This goes for you, too, scooter-ers and Lance Armstrongs. And wear a helmet.

minute until you can look at your phone again. You can make it. I believe in you.

* *Use your ears.* Plugging your brain into music or a podcast when you're running or walking does make your workout time seem to go by faster, but that's because it distracts your brain from what's going on with your body and—let's be honest— with the world around you. If you're deep into the zone, you're going to miss some important pedestrian safety clues— and not only the kind you hear. Skip the noise-canceling headphones and maybe keep one ear open.

## THE HITCH

—

**UNLESS YOU WERE** red-shirted for kindergarten, some of your friends will be licensed to drive before you are. Don't get too excited about saying goodbye to the school bus until you check with your parents. They may have some thoughts about you riding around with goof-balls who've had a license for less than ten seconds. They may also want to check with your friend's parents to make sure they're also comfortable with you riding along and to make sure it's legal—but you would never be the kind of asshole who asks a friend with a junior license to break the law, right? Once that's all set, there are a few things to remember:

1. Just because someone is a friend doesn't mean he's also your personal driver. If you need a ride, you have to ask. Don't ask too often. And no means no.

2. There's no such thing as a free ride. Offer to chip in for gas. If you're stopping for something to eat, treat your driver. In other words, return the favor without getting all weird about keeping track of debits and credits.

3. Get in, buckle up, and act like a civilized human being. Don't be a distraction. You could get yourself and your friend killed.

## DON'T BE AN UBER ASSHOLE

———

YOU MAY NOT realize this, but rideshare drivers are human beings. Before you get in the car, look your driver in the eye so you can acknowledge one another by name. You should do this anyway for safety, to confirm you're getting in the right car—especially if you're Ubering home after a night of drinking and have questionable judgment. Then, since you're in a car with another human person, don't do stuff like smoking, eating, grooming, or making personal calls about personal things. Don't be rude or use profanity. And there is One Essential Uber Rule that you absolutely must follow: If you feel like you're going to be sick, tell the driver before it's too late.

## *ASSHOLE DEAD GIVEAWAY*

### *Pukes in an Uber.*

*Bonus tip for avoiding possible lifelong regret:* If you think you're being a good guy by calling an Uber for a wasted friend, consider what's going to happen to him—or her—after the car drives away. Is your friend too drunk to notice where the car is going or if something seems off? When your friend is dropped off (hopefully) at home, will he or she be able to get safely inside? Are you sure? Better play it safe and follow the buddy system.

# YOU'RE IN THE DRIVER'S SEAT (GOD HELP US ALL)

————

I'VE BEEN IN the vicinity of a high school at dismissal time. I have seen things. Terrible things. Things no mother should see. What's going on there? Is it some kind of asshole driver contest? Two points for careening around a corner with someone's feet out the window, three points for spraying gravel, twenty-five points for the loudest stereo?

There's a lot at play here. Newfound freedoms, blowing off steam, impressing your peers—I get it. But here's the thing: None of these things is as important as you and all your friends getting home alive. I know your parents, teachers, and driver's ed instructors have already tried to impress this upon you, but I'm going to do it, too.* Every second you are behind the wheel, you are in a position to kill or maim someone. Even in a parking lot. Even in your neighborhood. Even at a red light. Inexperience puts new drivers at a disadvantage to begin with, so, rather than expecting your keen intelligence, natural instincts, and lightning-quick reflexes to make you invincible, you need to be extra-cautious. What I'm saying to you is the same thing I say to my sons and their friends every time they head out: Drive like a granny.

* *Grannies are laser focused on driving.* Do you see grannies fooling around with the stereo, checking texts, or taking selfies while they're driving? Never. Grannies grip the wheel with two hands, sit up straight, and think about nothing other

———

* I'm growing rather fond of you, dear reader.

than getting to their destinations. They're also selective about who they bring along for the ride—no more people than there are seat belts, and forget about Marianne. She talks too much.

* *Grannies don't take unnecessary chances.* Grannies don't change lanes to get one car length ahead or pull out into traffic when there's not enough room. Grannies take their dang time and go when it's safe to go, not a second before.

* *Grannies use their blinkers.* Grannies have their route all planned out and don't make any sudden asshole moves that might surprise other drivers and pedestrians. They use their directional signals well in advance to give everyone *plenty* of notice and a chance to get out of the way.*

* *Grannies aren't speed demons.* Even though grannies have far less time remaining on this earth than you do, you won't find them racing anywhere. Why do you think that is? It's because a lifetime of experience has taught them what's most important: getting there.

---

* Yeah, sometimes they leave their blinker on after the turn, too. Bless their hearts. Nobody's perfect.

## ADULTING 101:
## WHAT TO DO AFTER AN ACCIDENT

EVEN IF YOU avoid asshole behavior on the road, you may have an accident. I hope it doesn't happen to you, but it does happen, especially to new drivers. Accidents are a scary situation, so it's good to think about how you're going to handle things in advance, instead of trying to figure it out in the confusion.

- If anyone is hurt, call 911. This includes you, your passengers, and, if there's another vehicle involved, that driver and any passengers.* Once the paramedics and police arrive, listen and do exactly as they say.

- If no one is hurt, get out of the road so nobody *gets* hurt.

- Give your parents a call and let them know where you are and what's going on. Start by saying, "I'm OK," not "I've been in an accident." They'll be able to give you better advice if they're not in cardiac arrest.

- Approach the other driver carefully. That person may be hurt, angry, or confused. *You* may be hurt, angry, or confused. Keep calm. This is a good time to use your Bob Ross voice, not your Bobby Knight voice. If the other person is having a Bobby Knight moment, back away and quietly dial the police. Wait for an officer to arrive before you engage.

---

* Or, heaven forbid, pedestrians (knocking wood with fingers crossed while throwing salt over my shoulder).

◎ Exchange insurance information. Every time you drive a car, you should know exactly where your insurance card is. Let the other driver take a photo of it. Take a photo of theirs. Make sure you get your card back.

◎ Ask the other driver for a name and phone number. Make sure you write it down or note it in your phone correctly. Pay extra-close attention, especially if you're a little shaken up.

◎ Take photos of any damage and both cars' license plates.

◎ BE HONEST with the other driver and the police. If you effed up, you effed up. Don't pretend your brakes failed or your steering went out. The police and insurance people are good at this. They've seen hundreds of accidents. They'll totally know if you're full of it and were looking at your phone. P.S. Insurance fraud is a thing.

## GET ON THE BUS, GUS

———

WHETHER BY CHOICE or necessity, lots of young people take public transit. Buses, subways, and trains can have a dehumanizing vibe, because so many passengers hypnotize themselves with their phones to avoid interacting with one another. But no amount of self-hypnosis can change the reality that *you are traveling in the close company of other humans.* If you're a privileged young man, public transportation may be an eye-opening experience. Unless you're a total asshole, this is a good thing. It means your world, and your understanding of the world, is getting a little bit bigger. Pay attention.

Assholes act entitled and oblivious.

Non-assholes keep things considerate.

Good guys are observant and thoughtful about encountering a variety of new people.

Be aware of the space you take up. Are you standing in the door of the bus or train, blocking people at every stop? Is there a person using a wheelchair or pushing a stroller who could use a little extra room to maneuver or help across the gap? Could you hold on to the ceiling pole and let shorter people take seats or hold the handles lower down? Is there a pregnant woman you should give your seat up to? These are things that good guys do.

And can we have a word about your backpack? I know you can't actually see your backpack when you're wearing it, but I'm pretty sure you do know that (1) you have one, (2) it's on your back, and (3) it's bumping the person behind you every time the driver brakes. Why not take a step forward? Or—here's an idea!—take off your backpack and hold it in front of you where you somehow have plenty of space? Your passive-aggressive refusal to do so is making things weird for the woman behind you whose boobs are getting mashed.*

As long as we're getting personal, may I ask you a question? How can a young man possibly need more seating room than a grown-ass lady? Because that young man is a manspreading asshole, that's how. TIP: Look down at your legs when you're riding a bus or train. What do you see?

---

* Hi. It's me. Thank you for your future cooperation.

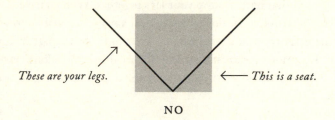

*These are your legs.*     ⟵ *This is a seat.*

**NO**

**NO**

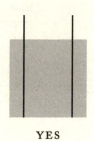

**YES**

FIGURE 7: *How to Sit Like a Person*

It's not that hard to keep your legs together. Women have been doing it for years, so we don't want to hear any nonsense about needing the extra room for "your boys."* Your testicles are part of your body. They don't get their own seat. Other things that don't entitle you to an additional seat: your coat, your bag, your lunch, or your trash.

| THINGS ASSHOLES DO ON TRANSIT | THINGS GOOD GUYS DO ON TRANSIT |
| --- | --- |
| Push or yell in a scary man voice. CAUTIONARY NOTE: Pushing and yelling gets people all riled up. Bad things happen when people get riled up. | Quietly say "Excuse me" and "Thank you." |
| Goof around like doofuses at recess. | Take up only the amount of space suitable for one human person. |
| Pretend they don't see people looking for a seat. | Watch out for people who may need a seat, like older people, pregnant people, or people with limited physical mobility. TIP: If you're not sure, just ask: "Would you like to sit down?" |

TABLE 4: *How to Act Like a Civilized Human on Public Transit*

---

* Talking about your privates as if they were people is a classic asshole move. Do not do this.

| THINGS ASSHOLES DO ON TRANSIT | THINGS GOOD GUYS DO ON TRANSIT |
|---|---|
| Take advantage of women's captivity, commenting on their appearance, making suggestive comments, or getting unnecessarily close. | Treat the women they encounter in the same respectful way they treat all other human strangers, rather than as prey. |
| Play games, video, or audio on any device without headphones. | Wear headphones and quickly turn down the volume when people give them the side-eye. |
| Carry on personal conversations at full volume, even giving it a little extra drama for performance value. | Realize that other people can hear their conversations and avoid talking about how wasted they got, how stupid their teacher is, their idiot boss, etc.<br><br>CAUTIONARY NOTE: Other people may include your parents' friends, your teachers, and your future bosses. It's a small world, and it loves gossip. |

TABLE 4: *How to Act Like a Civilized Human on Public Transit (continued)*

## A WING AND A PRAYER

———

Dɪᴅ I ᴍɪss a memo?

### MEMORANDUM

To:     Airport Travelers
From:  Assholes
Re:     Basic Human Decency

**Basic standards of human behavior are canceled until further notice.**

A trip to the airport has somehow become a *Hunger Games* situation in which every person is out for him- or herself, fixated on doing whatever it takes to get . . . what? A seat on a prebooked flight that is engineered to deliver all passengers to a predetermined destination *at the very same time*? I don't get it. Thought experiment: What if, instead of cutting down everyone in your path on the way to the Cornucopia, you acted with consideration for the comfort and safety of not only yourself but also your fellow flyers? Just imagine:

◖ If you have a laptop to open at security, or if you need an extra second to take off your belt and empty your pockets, you could say to the person behind you, "Go ahead. I'm not ready."

⊘ You could skip the airport burrito, clam chowder, or bacon cheeseburger before you get strapped butt to butt inside an enclosed space for a couple hours, and just have some nice trail mix and a soda.[*]

⊘ You could wander off to a less-crowded area of the airport to make phone calls so other people aren't forced to listen in on all your nonsense. I'm talking to you, Business Bros.

⊘ You could wait your turn like a grown-up. This means you stand there quietly, without craning your neck, glaring, huffing and puffing, bumping the person in front of you, or saying to no one, "WHAT is going on?"

⊘ Instead of venting your frustration on people who have no control over whatever terrible situation comes up, you could adopt a generally cooperative "We're all in this together" sort of attitude.[†]

⊘ If you see someone struggling to get luggage up into the overhead compartment or off the baggage carousel, instead of getting all huffy or eye-rolly, you could ask nicely with your inside man voice, "Would you like help with that?"

⊘ You could decide to never ever watch porn on an airplane. Ever.[‡]

---

[*] *See also:* taking a shower, wearing deodorant, and keeping your freaking shoes on. If I see your bare feet at 30,000 feet, there's a good chance we're going to be making an emergency landing.

[†] Who do you think gets earlier flights, better seats, and extra peanuts: assholes or good guys? Just guess. I'll wait.

[‡] Or in any other public place. Ever.

See, being an airport good guy is not that hard! One more thought: Even if you're a nervous flyer or you and your buddies are en route to a wild and crazy bachelors' weekend, you could take it easy on the alcohol until you arrive at your destination. That way, you can (1) be situationally aware and ready to use your man size and strength to help anybody who needs helping, and (2) not make the flight crew and other passengers twitchy about what idiot move you might try to pull because you're under the influence.[*]

---

MEMORIZE THIS

**Be a good guy on the train.**

**Be a good guy on the plane.**

**Be a good guy in your brain.**

---

[*] This is how assholes get themselves tackled and duct-taped to their seat. Don't get tackled and duct-taped to a seat.

# LOOK WITH YOUR EYES, NOT WITH YOUR PHONE

————

WHEN YOU THINK back on special moments, what do you recall first: the feeling of being there or the pictures you took? If it's the latter, you've shortchanged not only yourself but also the people around you, who would have rather focused on the experience than on dodging your forearm or peering around your screen.

Don't be that asshole who spends more time looking through his phone than looking through his face. Who are you "capturing the moment" for anyway? Don't say yourself. You're young and your memory is excellent. Is it to show off to a bunch of people not as lucky as you are to be at the beach, concert, party, or whatever? Because that would be a real asshole thing to do. Or are you legitimately sharing an important experience with someone close to you who couldn't be there? Again, no. If you were home with a pox, I doubt you would want anyone screaming at you over FaceTime from their amazing floor seats. Use your brain, not your screen, to take in the world you're seeing and to process how lucky you are to see it. Sometimes focusing on yourself is the good-guy thing to do.

# 6

# DON'T
# BE AN
# ASSHOLE
# TO
# WOMEN

**W**OMEN ARE HALF THE PEOPLE IN THE WORLD, SO IT would be really terrific—for both the world and for you—if you wouldn't be an asshole to them. First off, women have had enough of this shit, so there's a good chance your asshole behavior will be called out in real life or on social media with consequences of the career-killing and permanent-record variety. Secondly, women are not only your equals but in many cases your superiors, so you're going to have a seriously hard time getting ahead in this life if you make a habit of pissing them off. Thirdly, women aren't interested in getting naked with assholes.* Finally—and in a fair and just society this would be the one and only reason—women are people.

I know you know that women are people, but do you *know it* know it? Or has your brain been overwhelmed by garbage ideas, like relationships with women are some kind of game where the whole point is scoring, or that having sex is some kind of manly entitlement? If either one of these ideas makes sense to you because of stuff you read on the internet, you need to (1) get off the internet and

---

* Forgive me for presuming. It's absolutely 100 percent fine if you don't want to get naked with a woman, now or ever. What is not fine is acting like an asshole to humans you might be attracted to, now or ever.

(2) go to where the living, breathing, human women are and spend more time among them. Porn is another problem. Porn is to actual sex as *High School Musical* is to actual high school. *Porn is not real.* If you're watching it for tips and tricks without knowing how fake it is, you're getting some very wrong ideas.* You're headed straight toward a major embarrassment or disappointment—probably both, actually.†

Since generations of men have struggled with the concept of women-as-people, I'm going to go ahead and spell out some things that may seem pretty obvious. Things like: Don't grab anyone's pu**y. It may already be obvious to you that grabbing someone's pu**y is an asshole thing to do. You may even understand full well that un-wanted touching is punishable as a criminal offense. If that's the case, I'm sorry to bore you, but it's for the greater good.

FIGURE 8: *The Not-So-Secret Law of Attraction*

---

* Like, for instance, what breasts look like, how many people are typically involved, how popular anal is, how aggressive men should be, and how much action the pizza man gets.

† Studies show that people who watch more porn can be less satisfied in real relationships with real people. Who wants that?! That sounds terrible!

## WATCH YOUR BODY LANGUAGE

———

WOMEN DON'T HAVE the privilege of moving through the world in quite the same way you do. They have different concerns. For example: What do you ask yourself when you get dressed each morning? Maybe something like: What shirt do I have that's clean and still fits?

Your female peers may be wondering: Is this the shirt that's a tiny bit too loose so if I bend over some asshole might glimpse my bra and think I'm trying to flirt, or is this the shirt that's a tiny bit too tight so some asshole might make out the faint outline of my bra and think it's an invitation to comment on my body?

Whoa, right?

How about this? When your parents taught you how to drive, did they show you how to carry your keys between your fingers like Wolverine claws every single time you walk across a parking lot in case you should need to fend off an attacker? Did they celebrate your new license by giving you an adorably pink but illegal-in-some-states pepper spray key chain? I didn't think so.

What I'm trying to say is this: Be aware that your man status, your size, your strength, and the power of your man voice all have an impact on how you experience the world. Use your man status for good, never for evil. This applies whether you're romantically interested in a woman or not.

| GOOD IDEAS | ABSOLUTELY AWFUL IDEAS |
| --- | --- |
| Offer to walk a woman to her car. TIP: How would you want your friend to offer to walk your sister to the car? Do it exactly like that. Offer only once and without expecting anything in return. *At all.* | Surprise a woman in a parking lot. |
| Don't leave until you're sure a woman is safely inside her front door. | Stop a woman from leaving by standing in front of the door. |
| Say "Let it go" when you see a man giving a woman a hard time. | Hold on *even for a second* after someone says "Let me go." |

TABLE 5: *How Not to Be Evil, on Purpose or by Accident*

# HOW TO MEET WOMEN

————

THE BEST WAY to meet and develop relationships with women is also the best way to meet and develop relationships with people, because women are, in fact, people. You go places you like to go and do things you like to do. When you encounter new people, you introduce yourself, have genuine conversations, and decide whether these are people you want to get to know better. If you're a considerate good guy and not a clueless asshole, chances are that they will want to get to know you better, too.

## THERE'S AN APP FOR THAT

YOU MAY BE thinking: There's an app for this! There is! Lots of them, in fact. When you're over eighteen, you can try them out. Assuming you're looking for some kind of a human connection and not just using technology to locate the nearest available vagina, here's a little advice:

- Don't lie about your height, age, or anything else. Don't use fake pictures. The point is to meet real people, so be a real person.

- Start conversations by asking questions that show you actually looked at the other person's profile (What beach is that in your profile pic?), not by simply announcing your presence (Hey) or making a proposition (fruit and vegetable emojis included).

- "Are you up?" does not qualify as romance.

&#9416; Don't ask for nudes.

&#9416; Don't send nudes.

&#9416; **Don't ask for nudes or send nudes.**

&#9416; When you decide to end a conversation, say so: "Don't think we're a match. Good luck!" Only ghost if you have a good reason—not just when you get bored but when your Spidey senses are really tingling.

&#9416; Don't be rude. Don't be vulgar. Don't use profanity. Basically, don't message anything you wouldn't say out loud on a date in a public place.

&#9416; Don't be an asshole to anyone who's not ready to meet you in person or give you personal information.

&#9416; Don't invite someone you've never met to "hang" at your place.

&#9416; Don't demand an explanation if you get rejected.

Women sometimes want to feel sexy, but they never want to feel like they are *for* sex—that providing sexual gratification is their purpose on this earth. But you knew that, right? Because you're a whole, complex human being. Do you want to feel seen and understood and appreciated for who you actually are? THAT'S SO WEIRD. WOMEN WANT THAT, TOO!

Thought experiment: What if you kept your thoughts about women's appearances entirely to yourself? What if you opted out of locker room talk and hot-or-not polls? What if you never made any noises at all when girls walked past? What if—and this is crazy, but stick with me for a sec—you let someone know she is attractive to you by talking to her like a person you are interested in knowing *as a person*? Maybe she'll want to know you as a person, too! Could that work? Better than whistling and groaning when she walks by? Yes! I think it could!

### ASSHOLE DEAD GIVEAWAY

### *Introduces himself with: "I want to [redacted] your [redacted]."\**

---

\* **Don't** repeat any pickup line you've heard or seen anywhere, ever.
**Do** say, "Hello. I'm [*your actual name*]."

## USE YOUR WORDS

———

LET'S ASSUME YOU'RE not an asshole. You've met and gotten to know a real human person in a real human way, and it turns out that you have romantic feelings toward that person. A good thing to do next would be to find out if that person has romantic feelings toward you. There are a few ways to go about this, depending on your level of maturity.

| | |
|---|---|
| Grade school | Do you like me? Check one. <br> ❑ Yes   ❑ No |
| Middle school | Text your friend to text her friend to find out if she likes you. |
| High school and beyond | Ask her: "Would you like to go somewhere with me sometime, just the two of us?" |

TABLE 6: *How to Find Out if Someone Is Romantically Interested in You*

The last one is called "communication." It's best to ask directly, because this is a skill you're going to need again and again, especially if your relationship develops into something serious, and by "serious" I mean physical. To avoid being an asshole, do not say things or do things that the person you're interested in doesn't want you to say or do. You might be thinking, How the heck am I supposed to know what that person wants? You're not supposed to know. You're supposed to *ask*. Then you're supposed to listen to the answer. Then you're supposed to *believe* the person and act accordingly. When two people are in a physical relationship, we—and by "we" I mean police officers and prosecutors—call this process "consent." Maybe a few examples will help.

| WHAT YOU ASK | POSSIBLE ANSWER | WHAT TO DO | WHAT NOT TO DO |
| --- | --- | --- | --- |
| Can I hold your hand? | No, thank you. | Keep your hands to yourself. | Don't drop your arm over her shoulder instead. |
| Do you want to kiss? | I don't think so. | Back it up. Give a person a little personal space. | Don't ask again in five minutes: "How about now?" "How about NOW?" |
| Do you want me to take off your bra? | Yes! | Have fun figuring out how that thing works! | Don't get frustrated and go Hulk on it.* |

TABLE 7: *Sexytime Communication for Beginners: The Difference Between Yes and No*

---

* Bras are ridiculously expensive. It's all part of how the patriarchy keeps us women down. Stay calm and admit defeat. She'll think it's cute.

## TAKING NO FOR AN ANSWER

———

To summarize: You ask. You wait for an answer. You respect the answer. You don't whine like a baby, or beg, or make a big deal out of it. When it comes to a physical relationship, nobody "deserves" and nobody "owes." Nobody is "entitled" to anything.

*You* can say no, too. For any reason. Even if you said yes before. Even if it was your idea last time. You can change your mind about what you want to do.* Your partner can change her mind, too. After a day, or a week, or a month. At any time. It's OK. We're not keeping score here, right? And we know how to communicate, right?†

There's this weird myth that women want to be romanced, that they're looking for a man who never gives up, who goes the extra mile to prove his true devotion. Outside of eighties teen movies, this is called "stalking." Do not do this. If someone has expressed that she is not interested in a romantic relationship with you, do not keep asking. Do not follow her around like a lost puppy. Do not show up at her work. Do not keep messaging, commenting, or DM-ing. Do not ask her friends what she likes so you can surprise her with special gifts. All these things make people uncomfortable, not horny. Oh, and by the way, Romeo, other people with whom you have an actual shot are watching all this and putting you on their personal No Fly lists. Wearing someone down is not relationship goals.

———

* Real talk: Sex releases chemicals that give you love feelings, so sometimes it isn't until later on that you realize this isn't the right person to have love feelings for. An advanced good-guy maneuver would be to think about that before you become intimate with someone: Is this a person I want to love?

† Listening to the other person is important in your relationships with men, too, whether they be of the romantic or friend variety. In *any* relationship, be quick to take no for an answer.

## FORGET IT: YOU'RE IN THE FRIEND ZONE

⊘ "I value our friendship." "I'm so glad you're my friend." Basically, any major pronouncement with "friend" in it.

⊘ When meeting you, she always brings a buddy.

⊘ When introducing you, she calls you her buddy.

⊘ She mentions in front of you that someone else is cute.

⊘ She tries to set you up with one of her friends.

⊘ When you ask her on a date and she replies, "HAHA! You're so funny!"

⊘ She says no.

# ONLY YES MEANS YES

———

IN ANY RELATIONSHIP, but especially in a sexual relationship, it matters how you get to yes. Never use your body or your words to coerce anyone. If you feel gross or guilty* about how you convinced someone to get busy with you, doesn't that defeat the whole point of getting busy, which is to feel good? What you're going for is enthusiastic sexytime participation, not reluctant acceptance or— ABSOLUTELY TERRIBLE AND UNACCEPTABLE IN EVERY SINGLE POSSIBLE WAY!—fearful silence. Physical affection must be *freely* given.†

| THIS DOES NOT MEAN YES | THIS MEANS YES |
|---|---|
| (Silence.)<br><br>NOTE: Silence may mean she's still thinking about it. It may also mean she's afraid to say no or unable to answer. Any which way, it's a DEFINITE NO GO. | Yes! |
| I don't know . . . | Yeah, baby! |
| I guess it's OK? | Finally! Yes! |
| If you really want to. | Yes! I want to! Let's do it! |

TABLE 8: *Advanced Sexytime Communication: The Difference Between Yes and Not Yes*

---

* I am assuming you have an actual functioning conscience. Be aware that raging hormones can sometimes make more noise than your soft-spoken conscience, so please try to listen carefully so you can hear what your conscience is telling you.

† Free as in the person is exercising free choice, not free as in no money is exchanged. Please do not exchange money for sex.

Again, you have to ask. I know it feels funny asking, but you know what? Sex is funny! It's so weird and embarrassing and messy and naked already, what's the difference if you say, "Do you want me to touch you down there?"* If you're not ready to say, out loud, to another person, "Can I . . . ?" then you're not mature enough to do that thing with another person. Full stop. How often do you have to ask for permission? A good rule of thumb is: Don't head for the next base without making sure you have the go-ahead. But if you want to get really good at it, check in more often: "Do you like this?"

*Bonus tip for the avoidance of future doubt:* If you have any hesitation about whether your date or the Smirnoff is doing the talking, you're D-O-N-E. Done. You want your mind *and* your partner's mind to be *very clear* about when and how your partner consented, both at the time and the next day. It's not a good situation when people later disagree about what happened. If either one of you can't clearly recall these events tomorrow, you could be in for a world of trouble.

*Obvious but still necessary bonus tip:* Unprotected sex is how you get someone pregnant, so the same readiness principle goes for buying and using condoms. If you can't do it, you can't do IT.

---

* This is not a rhetorical question. The difference is you have consent.

# IT TAKES TWO
# (AND ONLY TWO)

—

So YOU'RE IN a relationship. How exciting! Tell me all about it!

THAT WAS A TRICK. Your relationship is not a team sport. You don't owe anybody the play-by-play. Sex is powerful, exciting, and pleasurable. It's also awkward, intimate, and embarrassing. Only an asshole would betray that intimacy by reporting the details or sending photos, no matter how juicy.* And cool it with the sexy selfies. Don't ask for any. Don't send any. Keep your gym shorts area a VIP, in-person exclusive. Once you hit SEND, that snap can end up anywhere. *Anywhere.* Trust no one.

---

Assholes are all about the nudes.

Non-assholes delete nudes without responding, screen-shotting, or forwarding.

Good guys may get to see an actual naked human partner in person.

---

* Don't be the guy who steps out of a bedroom at a house party and announces to the crowd what he just did and with whom. That guy is SUCH an asshole. Here's a much better idea: Be the guy who shuts down that asshole.

Sex isn't performance art. Don't do it in the back of a bus on a school trip, in the closet at a party, in a club bathroom, or in any other degrading semipublic space. Have some respect for yourself, for your partner, and for the deed itself.

Sex generally involves two human beings who are both having sex. Together. Only assholes think that sex is something another person does "to" them. Any particular favors bestowed upon you must be returned, and not some other time—right then. Both people have the same right to *fully* experience sexual pleasure. If you're not sure if the other person is satisfied, ask. Yes, more asking. But you're so good at it now, right?

Another thing about the two-peopleness of it all: Maybe you had sex with someone—maybe you just made out—and it wasn't good. Maybe you're embarrassed and want to pretend it never happened. Too bad. That other person was there, too, and that person is a human being. Pretending that person no longer exists in this world or that you never burped straight into her mouth doesn't change history. Don't be an asshole about it. Don't gaslight anyone. If you want *her* to be cool about it, *you* need to be cool about it. "Hey, so that was weird. Are we cool?"

# CAN WE STOP TALKING
# ABOUT SEX NOW?

———

YES, PLEASE. IF you've managed to make it this far through this uncomfortable chapter, you deserve some friendly G-rated dating advice.

Q: HOW SHOULD I ACT TOWARD WOMEN ONLINE?

A: *Like your genuine self. The goal is to spend time together in person, right? If you are the same person online as you are in person, you'll avoid all kinds of weirdness later on.*

Q: SHOULD I MESSAGE OR POST COMMENTS ON HER FEED IN THE MIDDLE OF THE NIGHT?

A: *No.*

Q: BUT WHAT IF I'VE HAD A FEW AND FEEL REALLY BRAVE AND INSPIRED?

A: *Absolutely no.*

Q: WHAT IF THE PERSON I WANT TO MESSAGE IS MY EX?

A: *Absolutely definitely no.*

Q: HOW SHOULD I ACT WHEN MEETING HER FRIENDS FOR THE FIRST TIME?

A: *Like yourself. Yes, they are judging you. No, there's nothing you can do about it.*

**Q:** DO I HAVE TO GO TO HER COUSIN'S BABY SHOWER?

**A:** *Does she really have to watch that boring show you're obsessed with? The answer to both is yes. If you want to be part of a couple, you have to do things the* **other** *person likes sometimes.*

**Q:** I JUST STARTED DATING SOMEONE AND IT'S HER BIRTHDAY/VALENTINE'S DAY/CHRISTMAS. WHAT DO I DO?

**A:** *If you're just getting to know each other, a card may be the way to go. Do not buy a card without reading it—you don't want to accidentally deliver the wrong message. Even better, go with a blank card and write your own thing. If you want to, give a small gift. If you're in middle or high school, keep it under $30. If you're older, spend less than $50. Don't get anything too personal. Flowers are good. Chocolate is good. But don't be a cheap-ass. Grocery store carnations or drugstore chocolates don't exactly say "I care." Better to just go with the handwritten card.*

**Q:** THAT'S . . . A LOT. HOW ELSE CAN I SHOW SOMEONE I CARE?

**A:** *Put the freaking toilet seat down.*

**Q:** THAT REMINDS ME! WHY DOES SHE TAKE SO LONG TO GET READY?

**A:** *Maybe she's been brainwashed by the patriarchy and beauty-industrial complex to think her actual face and body are unacceptable for viewing by other humans unless they are altered in a complex process requiring numerous chemical compounds and optical illusions. Or maybe she just likes spending an hour perfecting her signature winged eyeliner and red power lip. Either way, rushing her isn't going to help.*

## "TALK TO ME"

———

TALKING ABOUT WHAT you're thinking and feeling may not come naturally to you, but it's how relationships work. Sharing creates a sense of intimacy and trust. Someone who knows what stresses you're under can do a much better job of supporting you than someone who thinks you're acting like an asshole for no reason. Someone who understands your goals and how important they are to you can recognize and encourage your effort in a way other people can't.* But the biggest payoff is this: The more you let someone know you, the more secure you can feel in knowing they care for *you,* not for some front you're putting on.

You may think that acting "tough" or "strong" attracts women. News flash: Vulnerability attracts women! When a man shows us his true colors, we feel trusted and special. When he gives us one-word answers or shuts down, we feel rejected and suspicious. Which one do you think will get you more nookie: (a) trusted and special, or (b) rejected and suspicious?†

I know this is tough, because you've been conditioned by, well, everything—sports, TV, books, movies, your peers, the Olds—to "man up." It's not that easy to talk about your feelings, but nobody's expecting you to deliver an Oscar-worthy performance. All you have to do is act like your own true self, a human with human thoughts and feelings. So, when your significant other asks you "What's wrong?" don't reflexively say "Nothing." Think about it for a second

———

* Hey! Think about letting your parents in on the plan, too. They might not have a bouncy ponytail, but they want the best for you more than anyone and have more than a little life experience that might prove helpful.

† Answer (a) is the nookie one. But you knew that, right?

or two. Could there be a reason you're such a cranky-pants lately? What's on your mind? What were you thinking about just then, when she asked? Or last night when you couldn't fall asleep? Maybe, just maybe, that could be a thing worth talking about. You don't have to make a soul-baring pronouncement. Just make conversation. We're getting good at conversation, right?

Be yourself. Tell the truth. Let someone know you and love you. *This* is human intimacy.

---

### HOW TO TALK ABOUT FEELINGS

I'm not sure. I was just thinking about . . .

Nothing, really. I've just been wondering . . .

Nothing to do with you. I'm just distracted by . . .

Do you ever think . . .

---

## BREAKING UP

——

Not to jinx you or anything, but chances are you're going to have to navigate some breakups. Breaking up with someone doesn't make you an asshole. You're allowed to part ways with someone who isn't right for you. At the same time, getting dumped doesn't mean you get to act like an asshole. Keep these things in mind:

* *Be honest.* Don't make up some fake reason for wanting to end the relationship. Don't stop answering calls and texts, hoping she gets the hint. Be honest. Tell her it's over. No ghosting allowed. But don't say hurtful things or engage in some kind of post-relationship autopsy. There's no point in that.

* *You deserve to be happy.* Sometimes people stay in an unhappy relationship because they're worried the other person won't be able to handle a breakup. If you're afraid that your future ex will react dangerously—if you think she may harm herself in any way—you need to reach out to her permanent support squad and make someone aware of what's going on. I know you care for her, but you're not a mental health professional. Talk to someone (maybe her BFF, a school counselor, or a family member) who can activate the kind of help she needs. And obviously, if you're the one in the mental health danger zone, you need to stop thinking that keeping your girlfriend is the solution to all your problems and find someone more qualified to help you.

* *Don't talk crap.* You were in a relationship. You shared things. Secret things. Do you want those things broadcast to the

universe? I didn't think so. Give your ex the same courtesy and keep your mouth shut. You don't owe *anybody* an explanation for what went wrong. When people ask what happened, just say, "Nothing happened. It just didn't work out." Talking crap about your ex doesn't make you seem like a prince in comparison. It makes you seem like an asshole. And NO revenge porn.

* *Stop texting.* This is hard, because your ex was your number one fan, confidant, and friend. Losing all that at one time truly sucks. If you're lucky, your friends and family will quickly reenter the scene and fill in those gaps. Even if they don't, resist the temptation to continue texting your ex with everyday news, jokes, etc., "as friends." Communicating with your ex on the regular means you'll miss opportunities to connect with new people—there are only so many hours and Snapchats in a day. Plus, the inevitable mixed signals will be confusing, for her and for you.

* *You don't have to break up with everyone.* You met her friends. She met your friends. You all did friend things together. If you follow the don't-talk-crap rule, it's less weird for everybody and you get to keep being friends (maybe not from the very first second, but a little later on, if you want to).

* *Don't pretend it didn't happen.* Maybe the relationship was a disaster. Maybe the breakup was a disaster. Maybe you just can't deal with it in any way right now. That's OK. But, at some point, when you're feeling more like yourself, it will be a good thing if you give your ex a nod instead of acting like she was vaporized from her desk in English class. She still exists. *You* still exist. The world is still turning. And that's fine.

# 7

# DON'T
# BE AN
# ASSHOLE
# IN THE
# WORLD

I HATE TO BREAK THIS TO YOU, BUT BEING A GOOD GUY WITHIN a teenager-sized community is kind of easy.* As you gain independence and your world expands even further, you're going to have to work harder at this good-guy thing.

You might feel uncomfortable or anxious around people who are different from you. That's a pretty normal human feeling, but when it happens, what do you do? Do you puff up and act like a tough guy/smart guy/funny guy, spewing asshole crap to hide your nervousness? I'm going to go out on a limb here and guess that that particular strategy is probably not going to work out too well for you.

If you're headed to college, there's a good chance you'll be among a larger and more diverse group of people than you're used to right now. If you get a job, there's a good chance you'll be interacting with coworkers and customers from different walks of life. If you move out of your parents' home (go you!) you may end up exploring a new city, or a new state—even a new country!† Wherever you're headed, you're going to need some next-level good-guy skills to navigate the wider world.

---

* Partly because there are obvious consequences to being an asshole toward someone you're going to run into again—like, probably tomorrow at school.

† Note to my sons: Please remain within a single direct flight of me and your father at all times. And would it kill you to call?

## WHY BE KIND?

———

YOU KNOW THOSE viral kindness videos where an adorable little kid helps old people or soldiers, or maybe the ones where a generous customer pays the bill for a struggling family, or the transformational ones where someone living on the street is gifted a shave and a haircut?

Those videos really piss me off. Has acknowledging someone's humanity become so rare that millions of people need to click on it to see what it's all about? Is it such a surprising development that news reporters need to investigate and explain just how it came to be? I hope not.

*Don't be kind to go viral. Be kind*
*because you're not an asshole.*

You don't need to donate all your belongings and go live on a mountaintop to have a good life. Just treat other people the way you want to be treated.* It's not that hard to be decent to your fellow human beings. In most cases, it costs you nothing, except maybe a few moments of focus—and what are you looking at anyway, memes again? So why not be decent?

———

* There's that pesky Golden Rule again. Funny how it keeps coming up.

| REASON TO BE KIND | DOES THIS SOUND GOOD TO YOU? (CIRCLE ONE.) |
| --- | --- |
| It makes you feel good. | Yes |
| It makes the person you are kind to feel good. | Yes |
| It makes people around you feel good. | Yes |
| It makes people around you want to be kind. | Yes |
| If more people are kind in the world, more people will feel good. | Yes |

TABLE 9: *What's the Point of Being a Good Guy Anyway?*

## LITTLE KIDS ARE PEOPLE

———

LITTLE KIDS THINK big guys like you are the absolute coolest. They are fascinated with every single move you make, wanting to emulate you in ways you can't even imagine. If you think really hard, you might even remember looking up to a teenage someone when you were a Little.

Thought experiment: What if, instead of ignoring small kids drawn into your orbit, you took notice of the tiny people staring at you and said hello? What if you paid them a compliment on their helmet or kneepads or amazing work eating their veggies? What if you revealed the tiny-mind-blowing fact that you were once their same exact size? What if—and I know this is getting pretty crazy— for ten seconds you acted like a total good guy and made a huge impression on an impressionable kid? What if that kid were totally inspired to grow up and do good like you? Would that be terrible? No, it would not.*

## *ASSHOLE DEAD GIVEAWAY*

*Says the f-word.*

*In an elevator.*

*With kids.*

---

* Excuse me. This touching scene is just so beautiful. I'll need a moment, please.

## OLD PEOPLE ARE PEOPLE

———

I'M SURE YOU'VE been told to respect your elders. The reason the Olds are so obsessed with saying "Respect your elders" all the time is that we can feel your generation rising up to take our place. This is what's supposed to happen, and if we've done a good job in raising you, you'll do a better job of things than we have. But still, it's not entirely fun to feel like we're becoming both obsolete and closer to . . . let's call it permanent retirement. Plus, we have a lifetime of experience that may save you from making the same mistakes we did, if you ever took the time to ask. So maybe don't be so quick to disregard us as idiots, at home, at work, and out in the world.

Worse than being dismissed as an idiot is not being seen at all. I know that as we get older, we get kind of beige and harder to see, but we don't actually lose all human opacity, so you can spot us if you try just a little. So don't be an asshole and cut in front of us in every single effing line just because you can get there first.

*Just because you don't want to have sex*
*with us doesn't mean we aren't there!*

## PEOPLE WITH ALL KINDS OF
## JOBS ARE PEOPLE

———

AT SOME POINT you may have heard someone on Team Olds say something like "Every young person should [work in a restaurant/ dig ditches/do some other job that is definitely not writing code] for one year to learn the value of hard work." You might think your auntie doesn't understand today's web-based economy, or that she's some kind of sadist, but what's really going on here is that she doesn't want you to end up being the kind of asshole who disrespects people who put the *work* in *workforce*.

If you work at a desk (or plan to someday), this does not make you superior to people who don't. It doesn't prove that you are more clever or rich. It doesn't make you more important to the people who love you. Nor does it make you a better man. What it makes you is a guy who will probably need a gym membership at some point.

Working in the service industry does not make a person invisible, except to assholes. If someone is taking away your trash, for example, and you don't acknowledge that person, you're an asshole. That person is a human being, with a name—most likely right there on a freaking name tag. A good thing to do instead of pretending you're in the mysterious presence of an invisible levitating trash ghost would be to say "Thank you" while making eye contact with the human being doing something to make your life a little better.

Always treat the working people you encounter the way you would like to be treated if you were doing that work. If you were a fast-food cashier, would you like your customers to talk on their cell phones and gesture at the menu, forcing you to guess the order and whisper it back for confirmation, only to be met with more indecipherable waves? I'm guessing no. So put down your phone, place your order, and say "Please," please.*

## ASSHOLE DEAD GIVEAWAY

### *Rude to waitstaff.*

*Revelatory bonus tip:* In case you think this isn't important, I'm going to let you in on a secret: You know that it's important to be your best good-guy self on a first date, right? What you may not know is that it's important to be your best good-guy self *to your waiter or waitress*. That's right. Your date knows that you're putting on your best face and is looking for tells that you're an asshole in disguise. So, if you want a second date, don't ignore the human standing there waiting to take your order. Say please and thank you. Don't have a mantrum if the food takes a long time to arrive or if your order isn't what you expected. Don't do belittling shit, like snapping your fingers to get anyone's attention or making a huge mess. And leave a good tip. No matter what.

---

* Because you are such an attentive reader, you may be thinking: Wait, you said back in chapter 4 that working means getting paid to put up with shit. That's true, but cashiers aren't getting paid enough to deal with your shit on top of all their other shit. Don't be a shit-topper.

# PEOPLE WITH DISABILITIES
## ARE PEOPLE

———

I'm GUESSING YOU know that your buddy on crutches is still your buddy. He's hobbling around, kind of in everybody's way, and pretty grouchy about the whole thing, but he's still the same person, right? I mean, it's sad that he's out for the season, and his whatever-he-injured hurts like a mother, but he still needs to get to school, and do his homework, and get on with life. And he will. People will cut him some slack and help him out.

Guess what? People with longer-term disabilities are people, too. You may feel uncomfortable or sad when someone with obvious impairments crosses your path. It's a normal human reaction, especially for invincible young people such as yourself, because it reminds us that we're dependent on our physical bodies, which are vulnerable to injury and disease, which reminds us that we're mortal, which is kind of a major concept to grapple with when you're standing in line for a hot dog. Still, try allowing yourself to feel a little of that discomfort instead of somehow going completely blind to the person who is right in front of you or launching into jokes to defuse the tension, both of which would constitute asshole behavior. Then, maybe allow yourself to feel a little gratitude for your own good health and a little compassion for someone with less of it. Just like your buddy, people with disabilities need to get around and do their thing, so a little patience, please.

Some people would appreciate your help, say, with opening a door. Other people wouldn't. Luckily, there's a quick and easy way to find out whether someone would like you to offer a hand. Ask!

* *Would you like me to carry that to your table?*

* *Would you like me to get the door?*

* *Would you like me to help you on the stairs?*

* *Would you like to take my arm?*

* *Would you like some help?*

It's so easy, it's almost embarrassing you haven't already thought of it. But now that you have, you know what to do. No more excuses.

Oh, and by the way, you don't get to decide whether someone has a disability. People live with all kinds of differences, of both body and brain, many of which are invisible. You're not a doctor and you don't know *anybody's* whole story. What you do know is how hard it is to ask for help when you need it yourself. So go ahead and take people at their word about what they say they need. And if you make it a habit to be kind to everyone, you won't ever have to be that asshole who says, "How was I supposed to know that person had a problem?" TIP: Don't give anyone a hard time for parking in the handicapped spot because they look "normal." It's not your job to write up violations, so just move along.

# PEOPLE WITH LESS (OR MORE) MONEY ARE PEOPLE

———

Even as a young kid, you must have realized that some people have more money than others. Some kids had trendier clothes or arrived at school in fancier cars. Did you feel jealous and give your parents a hard time about not buying you everything? Did you eventually come to realize that they were doing their best and some people just have more than other people?*

People have or don't have money for all kinds of reasons, and you have no idea what they are. Some people with a lot of money have worked very, very hard for it. To others, it came quite easily. Some people without money spent what they had for good reason— boring adult-type stuff you never think about, like hospital bills. People face all kinds of circumstances that make it very difficult to get ahead. What I'm saying is that having or not having money doesn't tell you anything about a person's character. Only an asshole would think that all rich people are hardworking and all poor people are lazy—or vice versa.

All that said, if a person on the street asks you for money, you don't have to whip out your wallet.† You may not want to. You may have nothing to spare. Or you may want to help but worry that money isn't the right way.‡ Whatever you decide, this individual is a human being whom you know nothing about, so a little respect is in order.

---

* It's never too late to apologize for previous asshole behavior, by the way.

† Unless you're being mugged, in which case, hand it right over. Don't be a hero.

‡ If you're the kind of good guy who donates your time or resources to school or community charitable works, go you!

| ASSHOLE RESPONSE | NON-ASSHOLE RESPONSE |
| --- | --- |
| snort, scoff, or pretend the person doesn't exist | eye contact, nod of acknowledgment |
| "Get a job." | "I'm sorry." |
| "Do you know how much these guys make in a day! What a scam!" | "May I bring you a Gatorade or something on my way back?" |
| "Don't give her money! She'll use it for drugs!" | share food you're carrying |

TABLE 10: *How Not to Be an Asshole When a Human Person Asks for Money*

## *When was the last time you were charitable to someone other than yourself?*

## PEOPLE UNLIKE YOU ARE PEOPLE

———

HOO-BOY. WE'VE REALLY worked ourselves up over this one, haven't we? This little book isn't going to solve centuries-long religious conflicts or provide a resolution to debates over immigration policy. I'm just a mom, standing in front of a boy, asking him to just don't be an asshole. When you encounter someone who does not look like you, please try to remember that that person is a person.

Remember back in chapter 3 when we talked about *cognitive dissonance,* that thing where you don't quite realize your parents are actual people, and then they go and do something people-ish right in front of you and your brain kind of short-circuits because it can't compute how your parents can be your parents and also be people at the same time?

The same thing can happen when you make crappy assumptions about a group of people, and then get to know someone who's part of that group.[*] To rewire your circuits, you have to let your brain process the people you meet as individual humans, rather than on the basis of race, ethnicity, religion, sexual orientation or identity, or any other personal characteristic. This may not come easy. You may be surrounded by influential people with strong opinions about "others," based on assumptions or personal experience. Like most people, you probably have unconscious biases based on the barrage of stereotypes you've been exposed to. But you should try.

———

[*] Real talk: Being friends with one person of color doesn't make you not racist. The only thing that can make you not be a racist is not being racist. *See also:* homophobia.

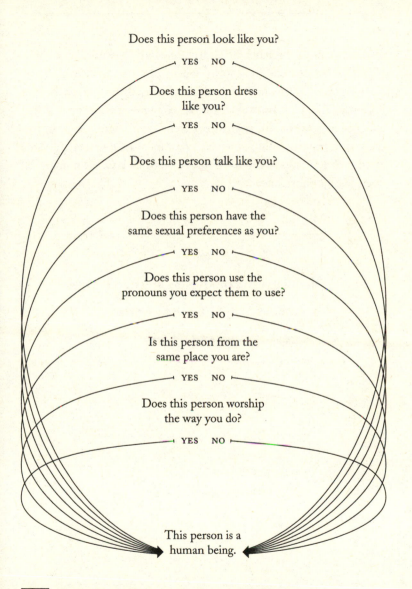

FIGURE 9: *How to Tell if a Person Is a Human Being*

It's going to be hard for you to enjoy all that life has to offer if you exclude whole groups of people from your own experience. You'll miss out on connections that can enrich you personally and professionally. Just think of all the amazing people out there! What are the chances that all your future significant relationships in this life—your friends, allies, romances, your mentors—will be the same as you?* You're too young to limit yourself this way. Be human. Be open to other humans.

**Assholes live in a small pond and never leave.**

**Non-assholes try not to make waves.**

**Good guys crew up and set sail.**

---

* The chances are not good.

## HOW TO FIND PEOPLE

———

ONE OF THE best things about getting out into the world on your own is the freedom to connect with new people. This can also be one of the hardest things, because it takes some effort to find people who are good for you and whose particular brand of weirdness you happen to enjoy.

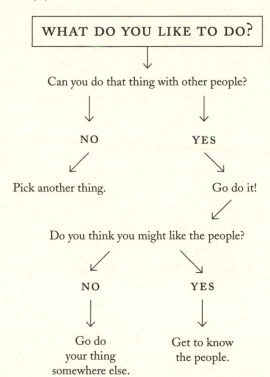

FIGURE 10: *How to Meet People You Might Actually Like*

# HOW TO MAKE
# CONVERSATION WITH PEOPLE

———

THE BEST WAY to get to know people is to talk to them. You are probably already an excellent conversationalist . . . with your thumbs. What you might need to work on is the art of making conversation with your face while looking directly at another person's face. Previous generations may have had more practice at this because in ancient times we didn't have email or texting or group chats. We had no choice but to withstand the horrors of unexpectedly encountering someone in person, blurting random weird stuff, and then running away.* People your age have had the luxury of avoiding people for vast stretches of time. But don't do that. Start putting these tips into practice now:

* *Introduce yourself.* Look at the person's face. Smile. Say "Hi, I'm _____." Stick out your hand for a handshake. One pump, firm enough that they know you're there, not so firm that it seems like you're trying to prove something. TIP: When the other person says her name, immediately repeat it out loud so you have a better chance of remembering it. "Nice to meet you, Jess."

* *Ask the other person a question.* Questions are the antidote to awkward silences. Ask something naturally related to the gathering, easy to answer, and/or likely to lead to more talking. Try these:

———

* Even with plenty of practice, I still do this.

— *How do you know [mutual friend]?*

— *Have you seen/read/listened to [movie, TV show, video, book, song, podcast of the moment]?*

— *Have you been following [sports series or news event]?*

* *Listen* to the answer; then ask a follow-up question instead of launching into your material. This will give you a little better feel for the person. It will also give that person a chance to ask *you* something, which magically makes you more interesting.

* *Give more than one-word answers.* If someone is talking to you, that person wants to know you better. If your replies are all yes/no/I don't know, you are giving the impression that you don't give a shit, which is rude.* You're also making it too hard. The other person will probably give up and move on before they have the chance to realize how interesting you are. TIP: Answering "Yeah" or "Nah" is a good choice—if you want to end the conversation quickly, that is.

* *Make eye contact.* Look at the face of the person who is talking to you, not in a staring-unblinking-creeper type of way, but in an "I'm listening to what you're saying and not thinking about peeking at my phone" kinda way. Nod—not like a bobblehead, but now and then, to show you're following along. Even if you get a little bored, don't glance at her boobs. Just don't. Even if it's for a millisecond, she will notice. *See also:* Women can

---

* I shouldn't have to explain this, but I've seen how you talk to your grandparents and aunties. News flash: They are also people, and they don't have to slip money into your birthday card if they don't want to.

always tell when you are paying more attention to the sexiness
that just walked by than to what we are saying.

* *Don't talk* too *much*. The following topics are excellent light
  conversation fodder, but other people may not find them
  nearly as worthy of quite the *in-depth* analysis you might think
  they are:

  1. your cryptocurrency holdings

  2. your podcast idea

  3. the band you're in

  4. the app you're working on

  5. your political views

  6. your workout routine and/or dietary habits

  7. the painstaking thirty-seven-step, eight-month process
     you are following to make something normal people
     buy at the store.

  As long as you remain aware that there is a human being
in front of you, you will be able to tell when you've gone on
too long. If that human is backing away, looking around
the room (for an escape), tightening his smile until it looks
uncomfortably frozen, going dead in the eyes, or blurting out
something like "Cool, where's the shrimp?" and running away,
you have talked too long. If you manage to take notice before
the shrimp run, stop talking! Say something self-aware, like
"Am I talking too much? Sorry! Tell me about something that
you're interested in." You'll instantly go from a blowhard to a
charmer.

* *No mansplaining.* Mansplaining describes the bizarre
phenomenon that occurs when a man ever so helpfully
breaks something down for a woman who already knows
more about the subject than he does *after she's told him that
she knows all about it.* Do not do this. Before you launch into
your manologue, pause. Ask, "Do you know [whatever your
manologue is about]?" Then—and *this is the big trick*—if she
says yes, pivot. Ask a question. "What do you think about it?"
Then listen and talk. Back and forth. That's called "dialogue."

* *Be culturally aware.* You may be downright curious when you
meet someone from a different culture than yours, but that
doesn't mean it's that person's job to educate you. Do not try
to guess someone's nationality or culture. Do not ever ask
someone, "But where are you *really* from?" Do not imitate
someone's accent or manner of speech. Do not ask to touch
their hair, clothing, or anything else on their person. Do not
offer unsolicited opinions on their food. Do not say you know
another person of the same background. Do not say, "Your
English is excellent" (unless you have just been informed
it's the person's fifth language). But don't be so afraid to
acknowledge your differences that you seem self-absorbed
or uninterested, either! If someone shares something with
you about their culture, listen closely and make genuine
conversation like a genuine non-asshole.

* *Be honest.* Listen, I know that it's normal for young people
to try out different versions of themselves. I understand that
meeting new people is the perfect opportunity to shed the
childhood rep you were stuck with all through school and
unveil the new, more mature you. I also know that if you're the

sort of person who gets nervous around new people, you might overcompensate for your nervousness by talking yourself up or even embellishing a bit. Here's the thing: These new friends are only "new" for a short time, and it won't take long for the truth about your Canadian girlfriend or famous uncle to catch up with you, which is going to really suck if it turns out you like these people and want them to like you back. Be you—the best version of you, but truly you.

## HOW TO TALK ABOUT POLITICS
## WITHOUT BEING AN ASSHOLE

MOST PEOPLE WILL tell you not to discuss politics or religion in "polite company." "Polite company" means people you don't know particularly well. This isn't bad advice but it may not be the most practical, considering that politics has become the elephant in just about every room. So here's how to talk about the news of the day without being a donkey.

⊘ Do a gut check on your own motives before you enter the conversation. Are you genuinely curious to learn about the other person's views? (That's a go.) Or are you looking forward to delivering a lecture or "winning" a debate? (That's a no.)

⊘ Don't ever say, "You can't possibly believe that!" No matter how different the thing is from what you believe, do not question whether the person you are talking to sincerely believes it. Instead, ask, "Tell me more about why you think that," or "Where did you read/hear/see this?"

◯ Remember, (1) people are complex, and (2) different people are different. The other person in this conversation has seen things, heard things, and done things you haven't seen and heard and done. Those experiences shape his or her thoughts as much as your experiences shape yours.

◯ Listen more than you talk. You might hear something you didn't know or something that surprises you. A good thing to say is "I never thought of it that way before" or "I didn't know that about you."

◯ Acknowledge areas where you agree, no matter how small: "I agree, this is a really tough problem."

◯ Don't beat a dead horse trying to find a resolution. When either of you starts repeating yourself, you've probably said all there is to say. It's OK if nothing got resolved. It's time to make it clear you're OK with it and to change the subject. Say something like "Thanks for talking with me. Are we good?"

# 8

# DON'T
# BE AN
# ASSHOLE
# ONLINE

Houston, we have an internet asshole problem. In forgotten IRL civilizations,[*] assholes had less influence because they were spread out and diluted among the non-assholes and the good guys. Sure, you would run into the occasional asshole, but they were easy to identify and dismiss, maybe with an eye roll, snicker, or disapproving cluck from your non-asshole friends and family.[†] Over time, these little signals would reinforce your asshole-identification skills and, more important, create what psychology types call "social norms"—the unwritten but well-understood code of things people should and should not do.

In other words, if you yourself had an assholey impulse, most of the time you could look around at the people you knew in person with your face, see that none of your friends or family were doing that assholey thing, and figure out that you probably shouldn't do it, either. Sort of like reverse peer pressure.

Flash forward to today. We have group chats. And sub-reddits. And 4chan. And only God and assholes know what else. No longer separated by geography or diluted by better influences,

---

[*] Such as video-game arcades, a place where now ancient peoples would gather to play Ms. Pac-Man and drink full-sugar sodas with plastic straws.

[†] Or, if you happen to be one of my unfortunate sons, a full-on debrief/lecture on the way home from every outing.

the assholes are cyber-connected and concentrated into like-minded micro-communities. This gives them the impression that their condescending, aggressive, hateful, ignorant, or other awful fill-in-the-blank ideas are not outside the norm. If in just a few clicks you can find a pocket of people who validate any terrible inclination your neurons misfire, it can be tough to notice when you've drifted into asshole territory. You might even get a warm-and-fuzzy feeling of belonging that makes you want to overlook the warning signs. Please don't do that.

Here's what moms like me really worry about: Even if you're just poking around the darker corners of the internet "as a joke" or to see what your parents are freaking out about now, internet assholes who seem hilariously pathetic at first can seem to "have a point" right quick, especially if your moral compass is still wobbling around, which is totally normal at your age. Be careful about what you let into your brain. Thoughts can very easily become words. Words can soon become deeds. Deeds are what make you an asshole.* So let's talk about how to spot online assholes and how not to become one.

---

* Less assholey versions of this little speech have been attributed to everyone from Gandhi to Meryl Streep as Margaret Thatcher. I didn't make this progression up is what I'm saying, but I fully endorse it.

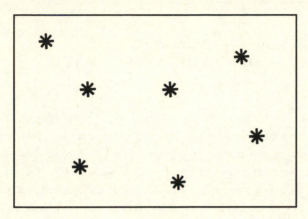

Assholes IRL

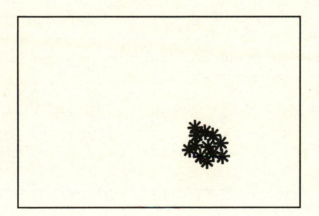

Assholes Online

FIGURES 11 AND 12: *The Internet Asshole Problem, a Visual You Will Never Unsee*

# BE A MAN OF
# DISCRIMINATING TASTE

———

WHEN THE OLDS were still young, talking to people on the internet was considered a good way to get kidnapped. Now we use the internet to summon strangers to our exact location so we can get in their cars. Online life is pretty much just . . . life now. So you should give the same consideration to your activity in the online space as you do in the parallel IRL human universe. In other words, cyberspace is not some kind of no-holds-barred Wild West in which you are somehow magically unaccountable, unaffected, and invisible.*

For example, when you find yourself in any new place surrounded by new people, whether you are in person or online, you should start by sizing things up and deciding if this is somewhere you should be spending your time, right? For starters, you don't belong in an online space if:

⊘ You wouldn't want your grandma to read the chat transcript.

⊘ You wouldn't want your little sister to meet your new "friends."

⊘ You wouldn't want the newspaper to report your presence there.†

---

* You are actually much more identifiable and trackable online. Surprise!

† Coaches, colleges, and workplace recruiters are looking at your online presence. You may think you have it locked down, but take it from a snooping mom: You are findable. More on this later.

In other words, if this subreddit/group chat/email thread was published to people outside the loop, would you have some fast-talking to do? It can be hard to tell where to draw the line, but there are some telltale signs that can help you determine whether an online community has a high concentration of assholes reinforcing one another's terrible ideas.

* *The only people in the bubble are people of your same age, race, background, etc.* It's easy to be with people you feel easy with. It's also easy for you all to accidentally board the asshole train while patting yourselves on the back and thinking you're a bunch of geniuses. Spoiler: You are not.

* *There are no women in the room.* Guythink will never ever produce one single bit of sensible advice about women. If you need intel on women, go where the women are. Hint: They're on Twitter, cracking each other up by making fun of the guys on Reddit.

* *People with different ideas are treated poorly and quickly exit.* You've seen this happen. People who try to introduce a different point of view are mocked, ignored, or just plain abused. Just like IRL, if you stand by and silently watch this happen, you are an asshole.

* *All the "jokes" are at the expense of people not in the room.* There are limits to the just-a-joke defense. Even memes and GIFs can be racist and sexist. If your go-to hilarious reaction GIFs all just happen to be images of people of color or women, give a long, hard thought to why those images are so funny to you.

* *The "information" being shared in the bubble is sketchy and/or all on one side.* Be skeptical of posts that may not be reliable:

  – memes, screen shots, quotes, or tweets taken from an original source that's not identified (for some weird reason, hmm . . . what could it be?)

  – "news" from sources you've never heard of, or only hear about in this community

  – reports provided without a date, author, or other verifiable link to reality

  – descriptions that don't match reports from any other source

  – tidbits that are sensational, play on your emotions, or feel like clickbait

* *You feel like you should keep your participation a secret from your parents and friends.* That feeling is called "conscience." Your conscience is an important check on asshole behavior, but it's a quiet, shy little thing. Take good care of it. Don't do things that make it feel bad or it might feel ignored and shrink away.

* *The conversation is so hateful or illegal that it requires anonymous accounts and secret codes.* Do I really need to explain this? If you are worried about being discovered in this corner of the internet, you are in the Bad Place. By the way, nothing on the internet is actually anonymous anymore, and, yes, the Feds are already there.

# DON'T BE A TROLL

---

IF YOU CRACK your knuckles and waggle your fingers to get warmed up before you log in to a social networking app, you, sir, are a troll. And an asshole. *Nobody* on YouTube needs your recommendations on how to improve their video. Nor do they need to know you think it sucks. Or blows. As insightful as such feedback is, you are not, as you might think, performing a public service.* Do you enjoy it when you think you did something great, or maybe you did the best you could at the moment but you know it wasn't great, and then somebody swoops in to pick-pick-pick it apart? I didn't think so. Guess what? People on the internet are also human people, so zip it.†

If you're more interested in participating in heated debates on Serious and Important topics like politics and religion, please know that, in addition to being an asshole, you are useless. People do not change their opinions on topics that impact their core beliefs after being lectured, cursed out, and/or memed by internet assholes. Social scientists have observed that people don't easily change their views even when presented with verified facts to the contrary, so although your cause may be righteous and your argument well supported by unbiased, truthful sources, chances are you're not going to make much headway.‡

---

* I'm assuming that you believe that your comments are useful, because otherwise you must intend them to be hurtful, and that is just too much for my delicate constitution to bear.

† Except for the bots. But they don't need your two cents, either. In fact, you're just giving them more data to work with. Let's make a pact not to assist the robot overlords, shall we? Thanks.

‡ I'm sorry about this. I don't know how it happened. Good luck, next generation!

Non-assholes know how to "read the room," an archaic expression taken from a time when people would typically engage in conversation with their faces while gathered in the same physical space. When the conversations are online, "reading the room" means thinking about whether your response is proportionate to the original post and consistent with the vibe of the group.

### CAN YOU READ THE ROOM?
### TAKE THIS QUIZ AND FIND OUT!

YOU'RE SCROLLING THROUGH Instagram and come across someone's Election Day selfie with the obligatory *I Voted!* sticker. Her caption is "First time voting. So proud!"

The top comment is a heart and an American flag.

The second comment is "Can't wait to vote!"

You are the third commenter. What do you post?

A. A thumbs-up.

B. Nice!

C. #BERNIE #BERNIEBROS #BERNIEBABIES #FEELTHEBERN #FEELIT #BERNIESANDERS and twenty-five American flags.

If you chose C, you are an asshole.*

---

* And if you put twenty-five American flag emojis on anything, I'm going to venture a guess that you are probably also Russian.

# DON'T JUST LURK THERE, DO SOMETHING

––––

**OH, HI THERE,** lurkers. I see you over there in the corner, watching this whole thing unfold. Did you think you were off the hook? After all, you're just quietly keeping an eye on various internet discussions, habitually clicking in to check out the show but staying above the fray, a mere observer. Good on you, right?

Wrong. Sometimes just standing there, doing nothing, makes you an asshole, even online. If you've misjudged an online community, or if a non-assholey community suddenly turns assholey, following along without saying a word makes you an accessory to the assholery. Mere membership in a community can be perceived as an endorsement of that community's norms.

Thought experiment: If this online space were a real-life party that got busted, would anybody believe that you were a truly innocent bystander who had just accidentally wandered in and had no idea whatsoever what was going on in the back room, or would you be swept up in the raid, thrown in the back of the police van, carted off, and charged along with everybody else?

Even if you're not worried about getting caught, what about your brain? It's a good idea to check in with yourself from time to time to ask whether the content you're consuming is good for you. What is letting these people into your brain doing for you? What is it about them that makes you reluctant to interact? Are there other communities out there that you'd be more comfortable engaging with? Be real with yourself about whether this is how you should be spending your time.

Non-assholes know when to leave an internet space. Good guys will say something first, then leave if the situation is not corrected.

This is especially important when the assholery is targeting a particular person or group of people, whether or not it includes you. You don't have to make a big drama out of it if you think going on the offensive will make you a target or inflame the situation. Keep it simple: "This is not cool. I'm out."

**Assholes are cyberbullies and their silent stooges.**

**Non-assholes exit communities that foster racism, sexism, or violence (yes, even in a jokey way).**

**Good guys call bullshit on that bullshit and tap out.**

## GAMING ETIQUETTE

—

IF THE PHRASE "gaming etiquette" seems like an oxymoron, you obviously need some guidance in this area. Read this quick, while you're re-spawning, and you'll be good to go.

*Don't rage-quit.* I've seen you trying to convince your parents that eSports are real sports. Can you imagine just walking off an IRL sports place in the middle of a game? Of course not. So it follows that if you're in a group gaming situation and you throw an online mantrum and quit, you'll leave your e-teammates at a disadvantage, which is an asshole thing to do in any kind of game. Treat your online game like a real game, suck it up, and play it out. You'll get more out of it if you can learn how to keep on playing when you have no chance of winning—just like in real life.

*Don't be terrible in the chat.* Don't tell anyone to drink bleach. Don't threaten to show up at anyone's house. Don't be gross to the girls. Cool it with the profanity in front of the kids. AND STOP YELLING. Just play the game and talk about game stuff, OK? You're blasting away in a virtual world, but you're playing with real people who have real feelings. And some of those real people have real problems in their real lives. You can't assume everyone will get the joke or shake off trash talk the same way you would. Just don't be an asshole and you won't have to worry about how anyone will react.

## *ASSHOLE DEAD GIVEAWAY*

### *Threatens to kill online or anywhere else.*

## LIES, ALL LIES

———

ONLY ASSHOLES THOUGHTLESSLY—or worse, intentionally—pass around disinformation online. I'm not talking about matters on which reasonable people can disagree. I'm talking about falsehoods and scams, particularly ones that can be harmful.

If something seems too juicy, too easy, or too good to be true, it probably is. Maybe someone made an honest mistake. Maybe the information was designed to be misleading in the first place. Maybe it started out as a harmless joke but got picked up by people who weren't in on it and took it at face value. There are lots of ways bad information gets passed around, so be skeptical and take a minute to evaluate anything before you pass it on, no matter how tempting it is to be the one who breaks the big news first.

Good guys do a little homework before they jump on the band-wagon. Before you hit SHARE, Snopes it. Google it. Check the original source. If something's not true, call it out. And do it before it spreads to Facebook, where your granny will see it, print it out, put a stamp on it, take it to the post office, mail it to you, and then call you to see if you got it. Nobody wants that.

## YOU DO THE NEW YOU

——

YOU PROBABLY CREATED your first social profile by middle school. You may still be digitally connected with your original crew on social media, gaming platforms, and other apps and sites. This can give you pause when you're growing up and trying out new things and new yous.* Growing into your new self can feel like you're rejecting or leaving behind your friends. This feeling is totally normal, but it's not a good reason to stay stuck in a version of you that no longer fits. Previous generations would do things like "strike out on their own" and "move up in the world." Cutting ties looks different for the first digitally connected generation, but the same rule applies: Don't be held back from taking a new direction because of what your online connections might think. The Olds have a saying for this: "Eff that noise."

If you've drifted apart from particular people, chances are that social media algorithms aren't showing them what you're up to anyway. You have hundreds of other friends by now and your old friends most likely do, too. But if it bothers you, don't feel bad about quietly creating a new profile or removing people from your online networks.† Another option is to just do your thing with everyone along for the ride. What does it matter if someone following along disapproves? Your life isn't an online performance. It's OK to move on. Just don't be an asshole about it: "Look at me now, suckers!"

---

* Here, "yous" means different versions of yourself, or personas. Not to be confused with the New Jersey plural for people, spelled "youse."

† This goes for people with whom you've lost touch, and also people who are not good for you right now.

## INTERNET HYGIENE

———

So BEFORE YOU got this book, you did some asshole stuff on the internet and now you want to be a good guy who follows the plan: school, work, life. Great! The first thing you want to do is Google yourself to see what your future coaches, college admissions counselors, and employers might find. Don't forget to image search, too. Oopsie. Is there some stuff that might get in the way of your good-guy plan? Immature nonsense? Incriminating photos? Posts that come off as racist, sexist, or some other kind of terrible?

- Create a LinkedIn profile or web page and build out a new profile so anyone who's looking will find something recent and decent that shows the new you in a good light.

- Lock down your social media by making it private, friends-only, or whatever the most closed option is. Delete any abandoned profiles or accounts. Delete posts that might come back to bite you.* Make sure your profile picture, tagline, and cover image are fit for public viewing.

- Change your social media settings so people can't tag you in photos or posts without your permission. If friends with unsecured accounts tag you, those pictures are findable. TIP: You can turn on notifications and untag yourself . . . orrrrrrrr maybe, just maybe, you should think about not doing photographable, postable dumbass stuff that can disqualify you from your goals.

---

* You might want to delete all posts earlier than a certain date. Nobody needs to see your middle school material.

## KEEPING IT REAL

———

Too MUCH OF a good thing can be a very bad thing. If playing games or being online feels more important to you than being with people IRL, it's time to reevaluate. As a general rule, interacting with people you know in person is more important than interacting digitally with people you don't know in person. After all, you are a human living in a human body. You need to do things that are good for humans, like eating, sleeping, exercising, and being with other humans walking around in *their* human bodies. If gaming or other internet stuff starts to feel like a compulsion, or if it's interfering with your health, school, work, or IRL relationships, it's time to take a step back.

*Bonus tip for aspiring-to-get-sexy humans:* Most of the time, human sex involves human bodies, so being around other humans generally increases your chances of it happening.

And then there's your brain. You only get one. The one you have now is the one you're going to have for your whole life, so don't be an asshole to it. Don't (1) fill it full of porn, violent images, propaganda, or other weird stuff that can warp its understanding of reality, or (2) get it addicted to the dopamine boost that games and social media use to keep us online so companies can get more money and/or data.

Something else to consider (with your brain) about your brain: Brains have limited processing power. If you're using all yours on gaming or other online activity, you're not using it on big-picture stuff like figuring out who you want to be. Getting to know yourself—your capabilities, your likes and dislikes—is a big part of deciding what you want to do* and how you're gonna do it. Your

---

* In this life, or even this weekend.

brain needs a little peace and quiet to deal with these important questions. Give yourself a chance to be bored now and then. You might be surprised what your brain comes up with when you take it offline.

Like kicking any other habit, getting off the internet can be tough, so try not to wait until it seems impossible. Maybe do it as a regular thing to make sure you're in control. Take a day off now and then. If that sounds crazy to you, you should absolutely, definitely take a break. Seriously. Like, starting right now.

*When was the last time*
*you took a walk*
**without** *headphones?*

## QUIZ: ARE YOU SPENDING TOO MUCH TIME ONLINE?

*(Select all that apply. And tell the truth.)*

⊘ You tried to swipe or tap this book. *1 point*

⊘ In face-to-face conversation with real-life people, you're the guy who quotes memes. *1 point*

⊘ When your battery hits 10%, you start to get sweaty. *1 point*

⊘ You have more log-ins than social commitments. *3 points*

⊘ Your best friend's name is something like "myxlplyx." *5 points*

⊘ You count leaving your room as "going outside." *10 points*

⊘ Waking up in the night to check your accounts is a regular thing for you. *10 points*

⊘ When you have a tough day, you *need* your screens. *10 points*

⊘ You lie to your parents about your screen time. *100 points*

⊘ You lie to yourself about your screen time. *100 points*

**1 to 3 points:** Take it easy with the internet. It's starting to get weird.

**4 to 10 points:** You're in the danger zone. Change your habits now.

**10 to all the points:** Your compulsion to be online is having a negative impact on your real human life. You need to do something. It will be hard, but it will be worth it.

# 9

# DON'T BE AN ASSHOLE TO YOURSELF

B Y THIS CHAPTER, YOU HAVE PROBABLY GOTTEN THE MES-
sage that people are persons to whom you should extend respect, consideration, and kindness.

Guess what? As it turns out, you're a human person, too.

You know how, when you fly, the flight attendants always say,
"In the event of an emergency, worry about your own asshole before
assisting the asshole next to you"?* Or have you heard the expression "If you're an asshole to yourself, how are you ever going to stop
being an asshole to everyone else"?† This is the point in your good-
guy journey where we consider a fundamental question, one that
your parents have asked you (or thought about asking you) countless
times:

## Why *are you being such an asshole?*

Maybe you have good reason. Your still-developing brain makes
it hard to resist peer pressure and exercise self-control. Hormones
can override common sense. Exercising your growing independence

---

* I don't fly a whole lot, but I'm pretty sure this is right.

† This one might just be me.

naturally causes some family fireworks. Or maybe those are just excuses. After all, not every guy your age is an asshole, is he?*

The thing is, wherever you currently reside on the asshole-to-good-guy continuum, you can do better if you can just:

1. Stop sabotaging yourself.

2. Let people help you.

3. Be man enough to say no to asshole behavior.

* This is not a rhetorical question. Please advise.

# WHAT'S YOUR PROBLEM, ASSHOLE?

———

THERE'S A LOT going on with your body and brain right now, but ultimately you are a sentient autonomous human with the ability to control how those changes impact yourself and others. If you find yourself acting like an asshole, ask yourself if it might be because you feel like shit. If it's at all possible, think about why you feel like shit and consider whether you can make some changes so you can stop feeling like shit and, hopefully, stop acting like an asshole.

### TEN QUESTIONS TO ASK YOURSELF WHEN YOU FEEL LIKE SHIT

———

1. *Am I sleeping enough?* You may be young and healthy enough to pull an all-nighter now and then, but don't make it a habit. Sleep deprivation is torture under the Geneva Convention. Why would you do that to yourself?

2. *Am I eating enough?* Your metabolism is faster now than it ever will be. Enjoy it while it lasts. If you up your training, remember to up your fuel intake. Look at what you're eating, too, and do better. It really does matter what you eat. Man cannot live by Hot Pockets alone.

3. *Am I coming down with something?* Do you have a headache? Muscle aches? How's your tummy? Your throat? Mmm-hmm. Take your temperature. If you're sick, stay home and rest instead of being that asshole who thinks he's too important to stay home and ends

up being Patient Zero, contaminating the population.
ATTENTION, PLEASE: If there's *any* chance that you
might have a concussion, get screened. Like, now. No
joke. Remember: one brain.

4. *Am I drinking, smoking, vaping, or taking shit that makes me
feel like shit?* Lay off and see if you feel better.* If you can't
lay off, you need to ask someone for help—someone who
has their shit together, not one of your drinking buddies.

5. *When was my last break from gaming/social media/porn/online
shit?* You might need a brain break to reboot. Give your
brain the day off. If that feels good, maybe give it another
day and see how it goes. If you can't give it a day, your
screens have become the boss of you. Talk to a counselor or
trusted adult. Don't be ashamed. It happens. A lot.

6. *When was the last time I showered and shaved?* If you have
to think about it, it's been too long. Clean hands, fresh
breath, can't lose.

7. *When was the last time I went outside?* Going outdoors
is good for humans and I can prove it. Exhibit A: It's
science. Fresh air and Vitamin D do . . . something to
make you happier and more focused. Exhibit B: There
are 70 zillion poems about nature's restorative effect on
the soul. Many of these poems are terrible, but still . . .
inspiration. Case closed.

---

* In addition to feeling physically better, you won't have to feel bad about any new
under-the-influence a-hole moves. Bonus!

8. *When was the last time I talked to another human person in person with my face?* Even if you don't feel like it, force yourself to get out there. Fake it till you make it. At the least, you'll get out of your own head and make a human connection. At best, that human will help you put things back in perspective.

9. *When was the last time I exercised?* There's always some new study saying how many minutes a day of activity at what heart rate are optimal; that's not what matters. What matters is that you choose a kind of exercise you like well enough to do regularly and then that you do it.

10. *When was the last time I did something fun?* Really fun . . . like the kind of fun you'll talk about with your friends when you get together ten or twenty years from now. That kind of fun doesn't happen by accident, you know. Somebody needs to say, "Hey, let's go do that thing we like to do with people we like to be with!" Do yourself a favor and be that guy. Everybody loves that guy!

There's a good chance that taking better care of yourself in two or three of these areas will make all the difference. If it doesn't, or if you feel so shitty you can't bring yourself to do even a little better in any of these categories, you may be depressed. Please tell someone who can actually help you that you may need help.*

---

* Sooner, rather than later, please, dear reader. I worry, you know.

## YOU MAD, BRO?

———

MEN HAVE FEELINGS. And at your age, those feelings can be powerful. But even if you're very angry or very sad, you don't get to act like an asshole. Rather than stew in your own rage juice, try to get yourself into a more productive frame of mind. Also, I would really prefer it if you would choose a reset method that doesn't have the potential to ruin your life or anyone else's.

| PERFECTLY FINE IDEAS FOR GETTING PAST RAGE | TERRIBLE IDEAS FOR GETTING PAST RAGE (PLEASE DO NOT DO ANY OF THESE.) |
|---|---|
| killer workout | drugs or alcohol |
| blasting music | reckless driving |
| creative pursuits | self-destruction |
| feel-good* entertainment | cruelty |

TABLE 11: *How Not to Self-Destruct*

It's normal to have a very bad day, or a terrible week, or sometimes, unfortunately, a really rough month or even a year. If your frustrating situation is temporary enough, focus on the light at the end of the tunnel and do your best to keep going.

---

* Clarification: By "feel good," I do not mean porn.

## HELP, YOU NEED SOMEBODY

———

**SOMETIMES IT'S HARD** to even keep going. Heartbreak, illness or injury, financial distress, upheaval at home or at work—these things can take some time to get past.* Don't make it harder on yourself by being the kind of asshole who alienates the very people who can help him move forward.

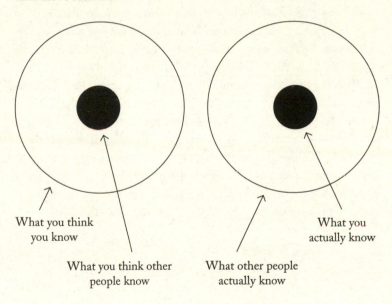

What you think
you know

What you think other
people know

What you
actually know

What other people
actually know

———

FIGURE 13: *Why You Should Let Other People Help You*

———

* Real talk: It's not fair when someone your age faces such hardship that his only choices are becoming a failure or becoming an inspiration, but I'm really rooting for you to choose inspiration.

To rise above a tough situation, you're going to need to start with a plan—not a vague, general plan like "Get a job" or "Do good at school." That's the kind of kid stuff you write in your kindergarten time capsule. I'm talking about actual-in-your-life first steps, like "Make a résumé even though I have no work experience and don't know what kind of job I can possibly get," or "Figure out a better way to study because I'm spending hours a day on this shit and it's still not making any sense."

Guess who knows how to write a résumé with no work experience on it? Every adult who now holds a job. Guess who has ten different ideas for how to learn the same thing? Teachers. And you know who wouldn't be the least bit surprised about any human problem and is excellent at keeping a secret? Nurses, doctors, counselors, and religious leaders. Even if it seems like you're alone in your struggle, there are people in your life who want to help you. Instead of acting like a standard-issue asshole and pushing them all away, maybe fill them in on what's happening so they can help you figure out how to make things better. Even a small improvement may give you enough relief to make the next bigger change, so go ahead and start reaching out. If you don't reach out, how can anyone give you a hand?

## REBOUND

———

**Let's be honest:** We're all a little bit assholey sometimes. People make mistakes every day. I do and you will, too. But now that you know what's what, you can't just pretend it didn't happen. So when you do blow it, don't hesitate to go for the good-guy rebound:

🚫 Face the consequences. Don't be a weasel about it, either.

🚫 Figure out who you hurt. Remember: It may be more than one person.

🚫 Make it right with each person you hurt, in a way that matters to them, whether or not it is easy for you.

🚫 Decide what you'll do differently next time. *Then do it.*

Things that don't help: making excuses, lashing out at others, giving up, and treating yourself like shit—even if you deserve it.

———

**Assholes make "mistakes" and try to avoid the consequences.**

**Non-assholes make apologies.**

**Good guys make it right.**

## MAN UP, FOR REAL

———

**BEING A GOOD** guy is not always easy. I'm sorry if you don't have a good-guy example in your life, I really am. If the people around you have gotten comfortable with doing things the asshole way, they may be caught by surprise when you first start to ignore their asshole suggestions and do your good-guy thing. They may feel threatened or judged. They may call you a wimp or a p***y. If they do, this reflects where they are in their good-guy journeys, *not* where you are in yours.

If there's one thing I want you to remember, it's this: *No asshole's reaction can change the good-guy thing to do.* So do it anyway. THIS is what "man up" means. It means you get to be your own inspiring, impressive, stellar example—and an example to others. Who knows? Maybe people are rooting for you and you don't even know it. Maybe some of your buddies secretly want to be good guys, too.

### *ASSHOLE DEAD GIVEAWAY*

### *Treats good guys like crap.*

# HOW TO MAKE GOOD

———

WE'VE COVERED A lot of ground here. So, in case your excuse for remaining an asshole is that being a good guy is just too overwhelming and complicated, here's a quick review on how to use your peak young-man handsomeness and newly authoritative man voice for good. I promise you, it's not that hard, and it's definitely much easier than living life as a permanent irredeemable asshole.*

1. Don't just stand there when an a-hole is a-holing.

    * "That's not cool."

    * "Not a good idea."

    * "Dude. What are you doing?"

2. Don't pretend other humans don't exist.

    * "Go ahead, you were here first."

    * "Excuse me. Sorry about that."

    * "Dude. People can hear you."

3. Remember that women are equally human, whether you are attracted to them or not.

    * "You read that article, too? What did you think?"

    * "That test was impossible. What was number three even about?"

---

* This list has four things. I know for a fact that you can name at least four Avengers, so quit whining and get with the program.

✳"Dude. You're just repeating what Hayley said. Give her credit."

4. Speak up when you spot a human with a problem you can solve.

✳"Excuse me. You dropped something."

✳"Can I reach that for you?"

✳"Dude. Wipe your face."

Be brave enough to be a good guy in the world, not just in your heart. Remember:

*Thoughts can very easily become words.*
*Words can soon become deeds.*
*Deeds are what make you a good guy.*
*Good guys make the world better.*

# Final Exam

*(to be graded on a Pass/Fail basis)*

## Are other people human?

❑         ❑

YES       NO

# 10

# JUST
# DON'T

| DON'T . . . | | | |
|---|---|---|---|
| get addicted to online gambling. | wear the same pants three days in a row. | forget to write a thank-you note. | fall off a cliff. |
| try heroin. Or meth. Or crack. Or acid. Not even once. | forget to wash your hands. | | lie. |
| cheat. | steal. | crash somebody else's car. | forget to call your parents. |
| say yes to things that make you feel weird. | | let your laundry pile up. | touch people without their permission. |

DON'T . . .

| | | | |
|---|---|---|---|
| kiss and tell. | | forget your umbrella. | pretend you don't care. |
| drink when you're already drunk. | be a mooch. | be a cheapskate. | live beyond your means. |
| forget family birthdays. | take d\*\*k pics. | | under-estimate yourself. |
| over-estimate yourself. | get addicted to porn. | tip your chair. | drag your feet. |

| DON'T . . . | | | |
|---|---|---|---|
| do anything you wouldn't want on the front page. | get a fake ID. | cough or sneeze without covering your mouth. | make promises you know you can't keep. |
| forget to floss. | hesitate to help. | act like it doesn't hurt. | |
| let your friends DUI. | | confuse doing well with doing good. | be a sore winner. |
| be a sore loser. | think more deodorant is a substitute for a shower. | wait for someone else to go first. | show up empty-handed. |

DON'T . . .

| | | | |
|---|---|---|---|
| get arrested. | get anyone pregnant. | take more than you need. | laugh off what you know is wrong. |
| fall asleep at the wheel. | | break a confidence lightly. | drink too much soda. |
| waste your life. | be afraid of being bored. | talk people into doing something they don't want to do. | skip the sunscreen. |
| go psychotic from lack of sleep. | text and drive. | | ever tell a woman to "calm down." |

DON'T . . .

| | | | |
|---|---|---|---|
| wait till the last minute. | stoop to their level. | expect someone else to clean up your mess. | forget to drink water. |
| rip anything open with your teeth. | wait too long to seek professional help. | be the guy who won't get out on the dance floor. | mistake hard work for good luck. |
| leave anyone hanging. | get road rage. | | forget to shave. |
| go down without a fight. | leave your people behind. | get run over. | get kidnapped. |

| DON'T . . . | | | |
|---|---|---|---|
| bite the hand that feeds you. | be mean to animals. | get rabies. | forget your manners. |
| fake it. | make assumptions. | | make things worse. |
| go out with wet hair. | talk more than you listen. | be shy. | forget to chew. |
| be too cool to have fun. | get roofied. | do crimes. | skip your flu shot. |

DON'T . . .

| | | | |
|---|---|---|---|
| take it too far. | give up too soon. | leave the seat up. | believe the sales pitch. |
| act like you didn't notice. | risk your brain cells. | drive like a maniac. | forget your seat belt. |
| take more than you give. | take it out on someone else. | | eat too much takeout. |
| beat yourself up—make a plan to do better. | go it alone. | forget who loves you. | **Just don't be an asshole.** |

# ACKNOWLEDGMENTS

First of all, I acknowledge that I can be a real asshole. But I would be an even bigger one if I didn't take the opportunity to say thank you.

Matthew Benjamin hatched the idea for this book, quite literally made it into what you see here, and got it out into the world. Monika Verma was the very first person who thought I should write it. Julianna Miner made for darn sure I did, every step of the way. Thank you and you and you, sincerely.

Thanks also to the mom squad for lending their encouragement, wisdom, and actual words to this effort: Lynda Ray Austin, Kim Bongiorno, Jennifer Barnes Eliot, the fabulous Amanda Hill, Susanne Kerns, Julianna Miner, Vikki Reich, ALEXANDRA ROSAS, Nicole Leigh Shaw, Alicia Steffann, Maureen Stiles, Emily THE QUEEN Tickle Thomas, and Becky Woomer. Your kids are not the only ones lucky to have you in their lives, you know.

If you picked up this book and looked at it for more than ten seconds, it was because of Jan Derevjanik's design. Thank you, Jan. Additional thanks to the Rodale team at Penguin Random House: Danielle Curtis, Ian Dingman, Phil Leung, and Terry Deal.

Thank you to these very kind people, who, when presented with some version of some portion of this book, pretended to be interested and said nice things: Bianca Bishop, Cynthia Conner, Rosalyn Linshaw, Kathy Miller, Sally Pasquantonio, Lisa Salerno, John Seebach, and Dana Silverman. Every single one of them thinks they didn't do anything, but they did.

Finally, thank you to my family. They put up with a whole lot. Obviously.

## ABOUT THE AUTHOR

—

**KARA KINNEY CARTWRIGHT** always says please, thank you, and excuse me—even on the subway. She married a total good guy and, through relentless lecturing, threatening, teasing, cash bribing, and tricking, they have raised two sons who are not assholes, for the most part. If you happen to know her in person, this book is not about you, for the most part. She lives near Washington, DC, and works as a law book editor.